FLORAL PINS

Simple yet elegant... these are a few examples of how to make a motif introduced in this book into a charming, one-of-a-kind floral pin. Choose stiff, mat surface paper like these or try shiny, bright colors, reducing or enlarging the size.
Be adventurous since variations are endless.

ABOUT THE AUTHOR

FUMIO INOUE is Chairman of the Tokyo Origami-kai Society. Ever since his childhood in Tokyo, he has been passionate about origami paper-folding. In 1970 he began creating innovative designs of his own, to complement the traditional styles he loves so well. He has introduced origami to young and old through lectures, demonstrations, exhibitions and workshops across Japan and around the world, including in the United States. He has also given origami demonstrations on television in Japan and has been featured in many newspaper articles.

Renowned artist Fumio Inoue uses the motto: "Origami from hand to hand." This describes his mission to pass on his art and ideas to others by direct demonstration, using his own hands. He is also engaged in a new project to develop special-paper designs. In this "BLOOMING ORIGAMI," he shares his love for the craft by showing how even a less experienced origamist can fashion these glorious flowers, suitable for all seasons.

NOTES ON THIS BOOK

The pretty 3D flowers being introduced here may appear simple at first glance, but you will soon appreciate the intricacy and ingenuity of the designs. Whenever you feel uncertain about how to proceed, be sure to check the following step(s) so you can easily visualize the procedures you should follow. First, prepare a sufficient number of flowers and buds; then arrange them using paper-wrapped floral wire and floral tape. Soon you'll have a whole selection of these popular flowers, and your personal display is sure to amaze your friends!

PAPERS

Begin with six-inch-square commercial origami paper, or any kind of paper unless specified otherwise on the instruction page. As you get used to the folding, adjust the size and/or stiffness of the paper and you will soon achieve exciting results — such as the examples shown above. You can also make creative use of different colors and pattern-combinations to give the flowers added vibrancy.

FLORAL ACCESSORIES

1 FLORAL WALLCLOCK

See page 38 for instructions.

2 FLOWER MOTIF

See page 41 for instructions.

3 FLORAL BOX

See page 42 for instructions.

4 DROOPING-PETAL BOX

See page 39 for instructions.

5 DOUBLE-FLOWERING TRAY

See page 40 for instructions.

6 4-PETAL TRAY

See page 44 for instructions.

SEASONAL FLOWERS

7 CHERRY BLOSSOMS

See page 45 for instructions.

8 DOGWOOD BLOSSOMS

See page 46 for instructions.

9 PANSY

See page 67 for instructions.

10 VIOLET

See page 48 for instructions.

11 SWEET PEA

See page 50 for instructions.

12 TULIP
See page 71 for instructions.

13 LILY OF THE VALLEY

See page 52 for instructions.

14 CARNATION
See page 54 for instructions.

15 ROSE

See page 56 for instructions.

16 CLIMBING ROSE

See page 58 for instructions.

17 JAPANESE IRIS
See page 60 for instructions.

18 HELMET
See page 62 for instructions.

14

19 HYDRANGEA

See page 63 for instructions.

20 MORNING GLORY

See page 64 for instructions.

21 6-PETAL CLEMATIS

See page 70 for instructions.

22 8-PETAL CLEMATIS

See page 68 for instructions.

23 BOUGAINVILLEA
See page 72 for instructions.

24 6-PETAL LILY
See page 74 for instructions.

25 LILY
(TRADITIONAL FOLDING)
See page 76 for instructions.

SUMMER

26 SUNFLOWER
See page 78 for instructions.

27 DAHLIA
See page 80 for instructions.

28 5-PETAL GENTIAN

See page 84 for instructions.

29 4-PETAL GENTIAN

See page 82 for instructions.

31 5-PETAL BALLOONFLOWER
See page 88 for instructions.

30 4-PETAL BALLOONFLOWER
See page 86 for instructions.

23

AUTUMN

32 CHRYSANTHEMUM
See page 85 for instructions.

33 EVENING PRIMROSE

See page 90 for instructions.

34 ADONIS FLOWER

See page 92 for instructions.

35 DAFFODIL
See page 77 for instructions.

Side View

27

36 CAMELLIA

See page 94 for instructions.

37 TREE PEONY
See page 102 for instructions.

38 KAFFIR LILY

See page 96 for instructions.

39 CYCLAMEN

See page 98 for instructions.

40 PHALAENOPSIS ORCHID
See page 100 for instructions.

ORIGAMI SYMBOLS Fold carefully checking dotted lines and arrows.

Colored side (Right Side)

RS

White side (Wrong Side)

WS

Mountain fold —·—·—·—·—

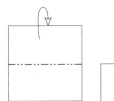

Valley fold — — — — —

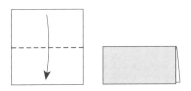

Turn over.

Crease. (Fold and unfold.)

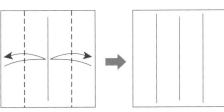

Existing crease

Fold over and over. (Roll.)

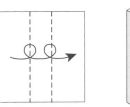

Turn around.

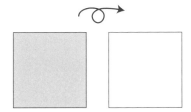

Step-fold (Pleat fold)

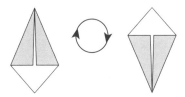

Reverse fold

Inside Reverse Fold (Tucking in mountain fold)

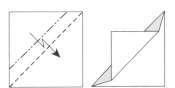

Outside Reverse Fold (Unfold and fold over.)

Enlarging and Reducing

Enlarging

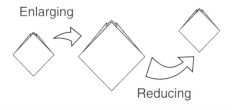

Reducing

Pull out.

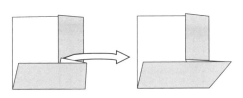

Insert.

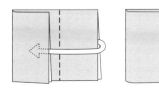

Push inside.

Crease.

Push and fold.

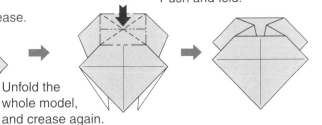

Unfold the whole model, and crease again.

Lift. (Insert your fingers.)

Squash-fold from the top.

33

This base is also called a preliminary base or bird base.
There are three methods to make this, and all of them result in the same form.

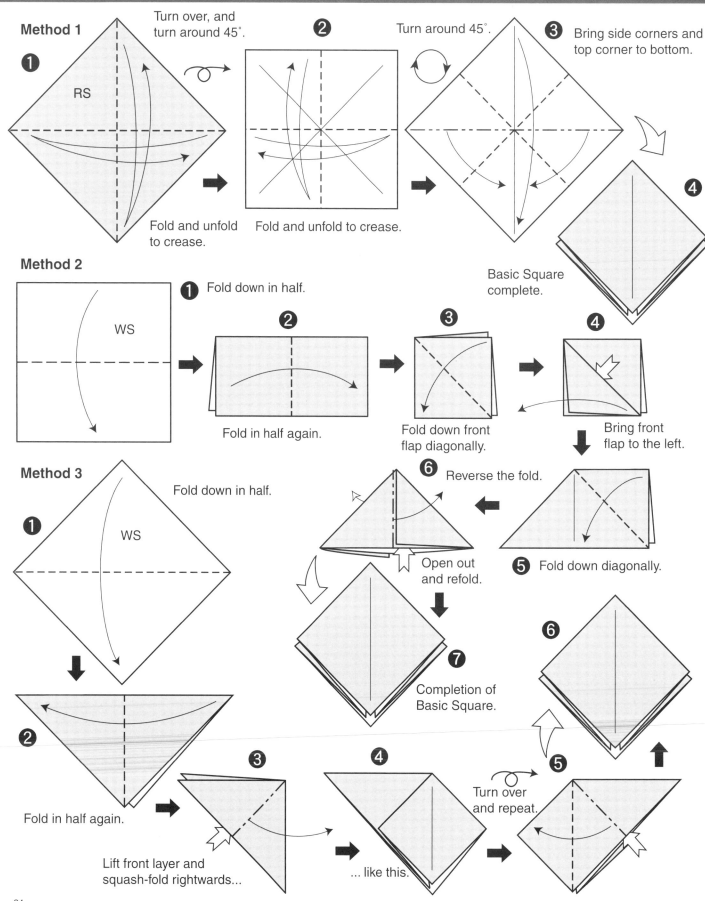

Method 1

1 RS

Turn over, and turn around 45°.

Fold and unfold to crease.

2 Turn around 45°.

Fold and unfold to crease.

3 Bring side corners and top corner to bottom.

4 Basic Square complete.

Method 2

WS

1 Fold down in half.

2 Fold in half again.

3 Fold down front flap diagonally.

4 Bring front flap to the left.

5 Fold down diagonally.

6 Reverse the fold.

Open out and refold.

7 Completion of Basic Square.

Method 3

1 WS

Fold down in half.

2 Fold in half again.

3 Lift front layer and squash-fold rightwards...

4 ... like this.

5 Turn over and repeat.

6

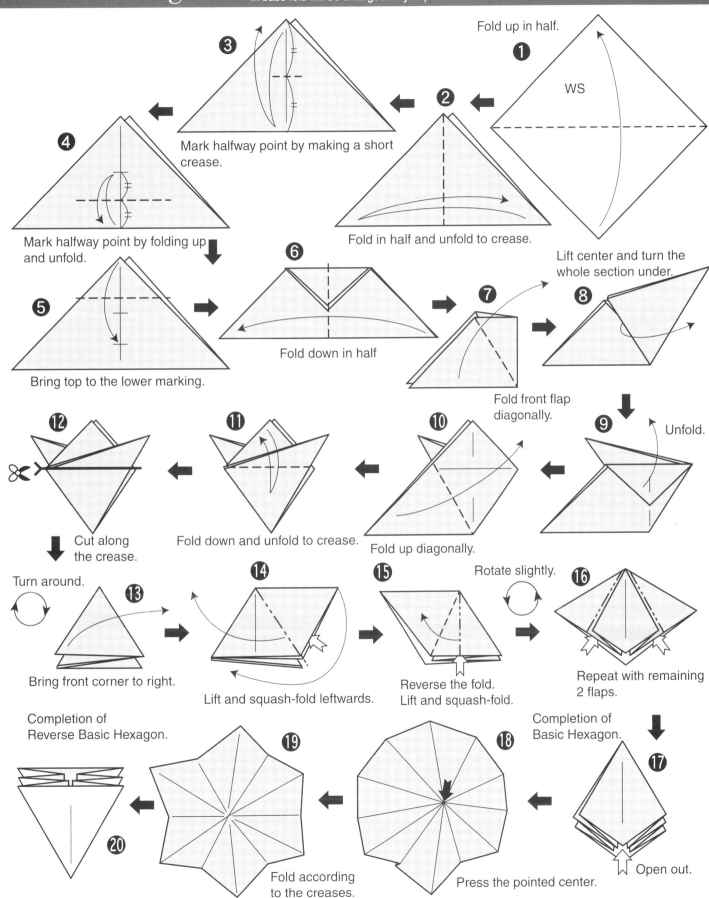

❶ Fold up in half.

WS

❷ Fold in half and unfold to crease.

❸ Mark halfway point by making a short crease.

❹ Mark halfway point by folding up and unfold.

❺ Bring top to the lower marking.

❻ Fold down in half

❼ Fold front flap diagonally.

❽ Lift center and turn the whole section under.

❾ Unfold.

❿ Fold up diagonally.

⓫ Fold down and unfold to crease.

⓬ Cut along the crease.

Turn around.

⓭ Bring front corner to right.

⓮ Lift and squash-fold leftwards.

⓯ Reverse the fold. Lift and squash-fold.

Rotate slightly.

⓰ Repeat with remaining 2 flaps.

Completion of Basic Hexagon.

⓱ Open out.

⓲ Press the pointed center.

⓳ Fold according to the creases.

Completion of Reverse Basic Hexagon.

⓴

35

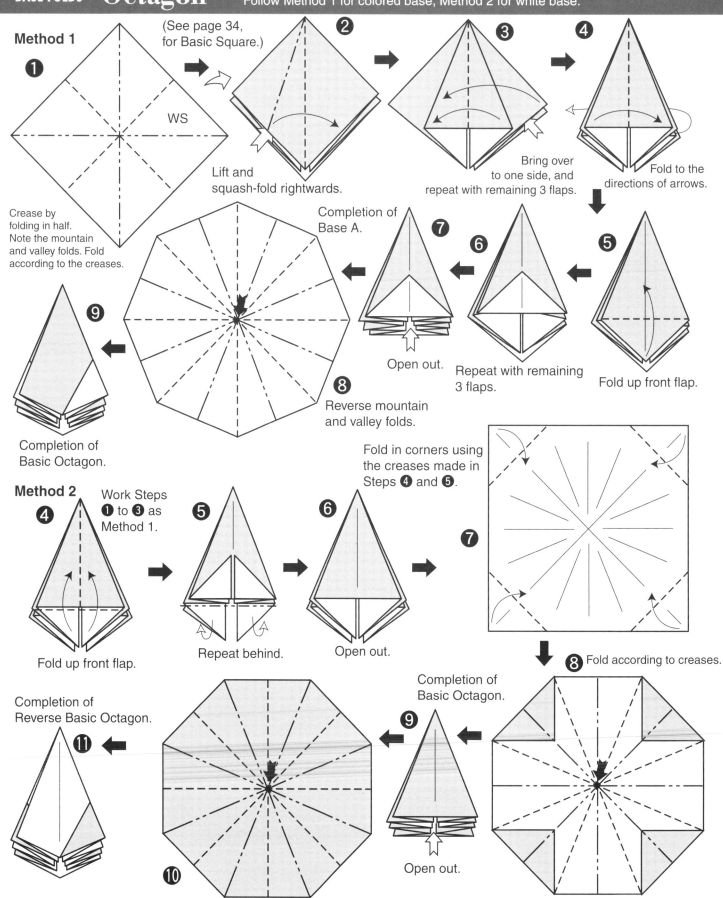

Method 1

1

(See page 34, for Basic Square.)

WS

Crease by folding in half. Note the mountain and valley folds. Fold according to the creases.

2

Lift and squash-fold rightwards.

3

Bring over to one side, and repeat with remaining 3 flaps.

4

Fold to the directions of arrows.

5

Fold up front flap.

6

Repeat with remaining 3 flaps.

7

Open out.

Completion of Base A.

8

Reverse mountain and valley folds.

9

Completion of Basic Octagon.

Method 2

4

Work Steps **1** to **3** as Method 1.

Fold up front flap.

5

Repeat behind.

6

Open out.

7

Fold in corners using the creases made in Steps **4** and **5**.

8 Fold according to creases.

9

Completion of Basic Octagon.

Open out.

10

Press the pointed center and fold accordingly.

11

Completion of Reverse Basic Octagon.

36

For a perfect origami, it is essential to make accurate creases at this stage. A small difference in base fold will be enlarged as you proceed.

1 Fold up in half.

WS

2 Fold in half and unfold.

3 Mark halfway point by making a short crease.

4 Fold down top corners.

5 Fold in half.

6 Bring front flap over to left.

Bring left edge to center fold.

7

8 Turn over.

9 Bring over to left.

10 Unfold.

11 Fold to align with back side.

12 Fold left edge to right.

13 Crease.

14 Trim away.

15 Pull front and back flap to sides.

Turn around.

16 Lift and squash leftwards.

17 Repeat.

18 Turn over.

19 Lift and squash leftwards.

Completion of Basic Pentagon.

20

21

22 Fold according to creases.

Press down pointed center.

Completion of Reverse Basic Pentagon.

23

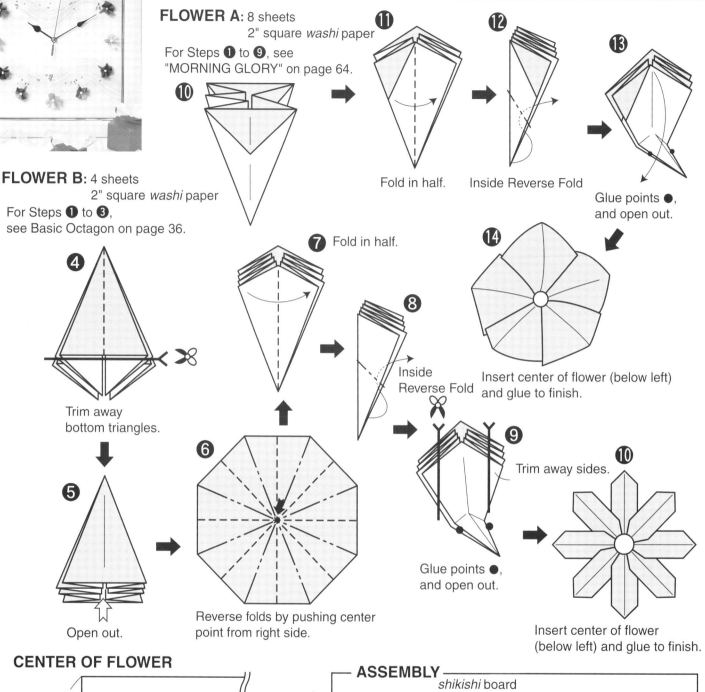

FLOWER A: 8 sheets
2" square *washi* paper

For Steps ❶ to ❾, see
"MORNING GLORY" on page 64.

❿

⓫ Fold in half.

⓬ Inside Reverse Fold

⓭ Glue points ●, and open out.

⓮ Insert center of flower (below left) and glue to finish.

FLOWER B: 4 sheets
2" square *washi* paper

For Steps ❶ to ❸,
see Basic Octagon on page 36.

❹ Trim away bottom triangles.

❺ Open out.

❻ Reverse folds by pushing center point from right side.

❼ Fold in half.

❽ Inside Reverse Fold

❾ Glue points ●, and open out.

Trim away sides.

❿ Insert center of flower (below left) and glue to finish.

CENTER OF FLOWER

approx. 1"   yellow *washi*

Crumple.   ¼"   ¼"   ⅛"   Roll up.

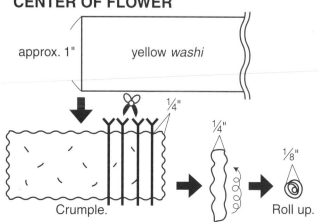

ASSEMBLY

shikishi board

Install clock movement and hands at the center of board. Glue flowers onto positions so that hands do not touch.

11"

9½"

A B A
A A
B B
A A
A B A

Point to center.

Glue bottom. (seen from the side)

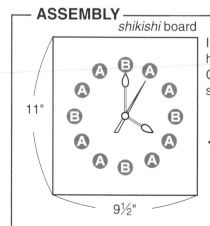

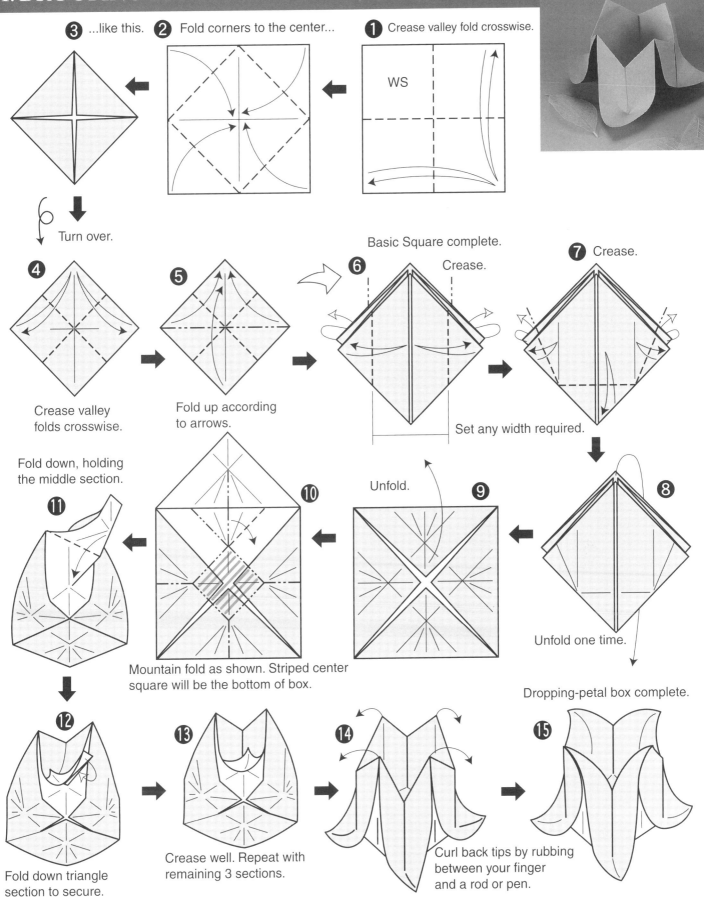

③ ...like this. **②** Fold corners to the center... **①** Crease valley fold crosswise.

WS

Turn over.

Basic Square complete.

Crease.

⑦ Crease.

④ Crease valley folds crosswise.

⑤ Fold up according to arrows.

⑥ Set any width required.

⑧ Unfold one time.

Dropping-petal box complete.

⑨ Unfold.

⑩ Mountain fold as shown. Striped center square will be the bottom of box.

⑪ Fold down, holding the middle section.

⑫ Fold down triangle section to secure.

⑬ Crease well. Repeat with remaining 3 sections.

⑭ Curl back tips by rubbing between your finger and a rod or pen.

⑮

5. DOUBLE-FLOWERING TRAY shown on page 3 6" double-sided origami

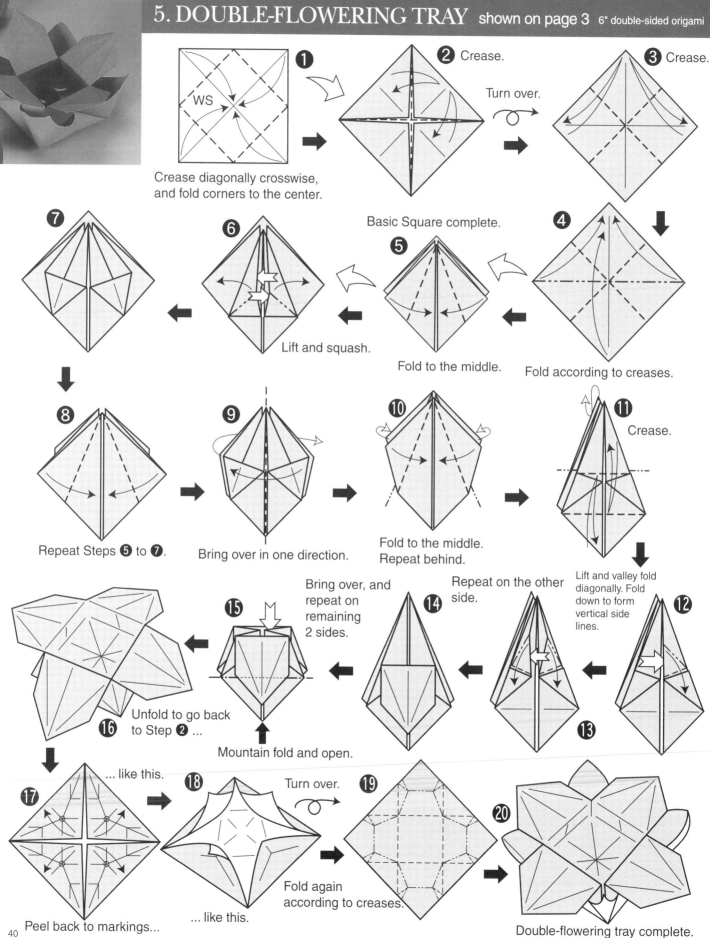

1 Crease diagonally crosswise, and fold corners to the center.

2 Crease. Turn over.

3 Crease.

4 Fold according to creases.

5 Fold to the middle.

Basic Square complete.

6 Lift and squash.

7

8 Repeat Steps 5 to 7.

9 Bring over in one direction.

10 Fold to the middle. Repeat behind.

11 Crease.

12 Lift and valley fold diagonally. Fold down to form vertical side lines.

13

14 Repeat on the other side.

15 Bring over, and repeat on remaining 2 sides.

Mountain fold and open.

16 Unfold to go back to Step 2 ...

17 Peel back to markings... ... like this.

18 ... like this.

Turn over.

19 Fold again according to creases.

20 Double-flowering tray complete.

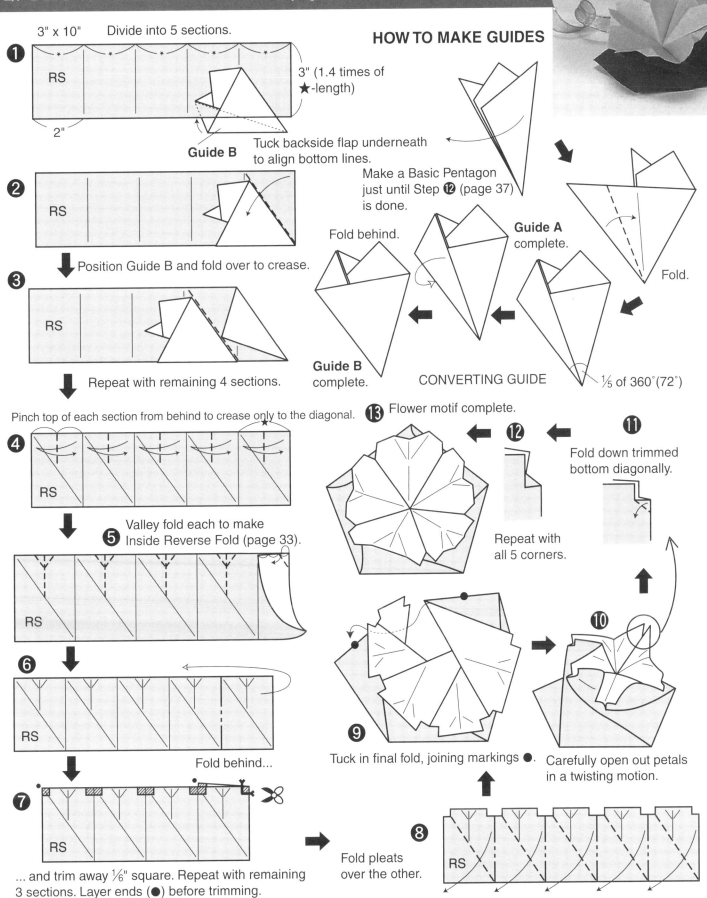

HOW TO MAKE GUIDES

❶ 3" x 10"   Divide into 5 sections.

RS

2"

3" (1.4 times of ★-length)

Guide B

Tuck backside flap underneath to align bottom lines.

Make a Basic Pentagon just until Step ⑫ (page 37) is done.

Fold behind.

Guide A complete.

Fold.

❷ RS

Position Guide B and fold over to crease.

❸ RS

Repeat with remaining 4 sections.

Guide B complete.

CONVERTING GUIDE

⅕ of 360°(72°)

Pinch top of each section from behind to crease only to the diagonal.

❹ RS

❸ Flower motif complete.

⑫

⑪

Fold down trimmed bottom diagonally.

Valley fold each to make
❺ Inside Reverse Fold (page 33).

RS

Repeat with all 5 corners.

❻ RS

⑩

Fold behind...

❼ RS

... and trim away ⅙" square. Repeat with remaining 3 sections. Layer ends (●) before trimming.

❾

Tuck in final fold, joining markings ●.

Carefully open out petals in a twisting motion.

Fold pleats over the other.

❽ RS

41

3. FLORAL BOX shown on page 2

For easy comprehension, it is recommended to practice "FLOWER MOTIF" before making this model.

See page 41 for Guides A and B.

❶ Use stiff and thick rectangular sheet of paper. Leaving ½" allowance on a short side, and divide remaining length into 5 equal parts.

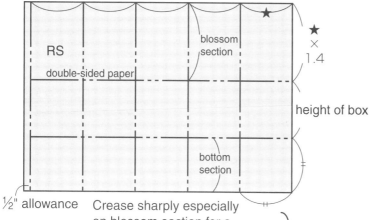

RS
double-sided paper

blossom section

★

★ × 1.4

height of box

bottom section

½" allowance

Crease sharply especially on blossom section for a good result.

❷ Begin with the bottom.

WS

bottom section

Re-form creases of marking ◎ into mountain folds.

Valley fold between markings ■ to form an L-shape.

❸

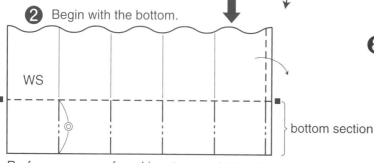

WS

Guide A

Make Guide A and position as shown. Bring over to crease.

❹

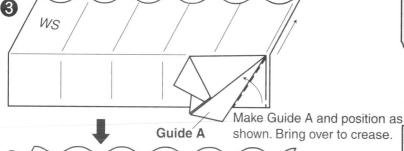

WS

Repeat with remaining 4 squares.

Turn over.

❿ Repeat with remaining 4 squares.

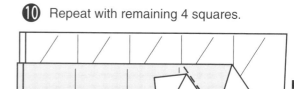

RS

❾ Valley fold diagonally.

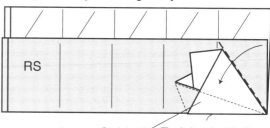

RS

Guide B Tuck backside flap underneath to align bottom lines.

❽

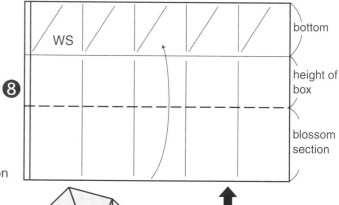

WS

bottom

height of box

blossom section

❻ .. until a box shape is formed.

❼ Keep this model in mind, and unfold.

❺ Fold pleats over the other...

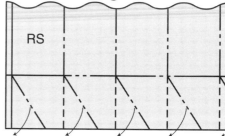

RS

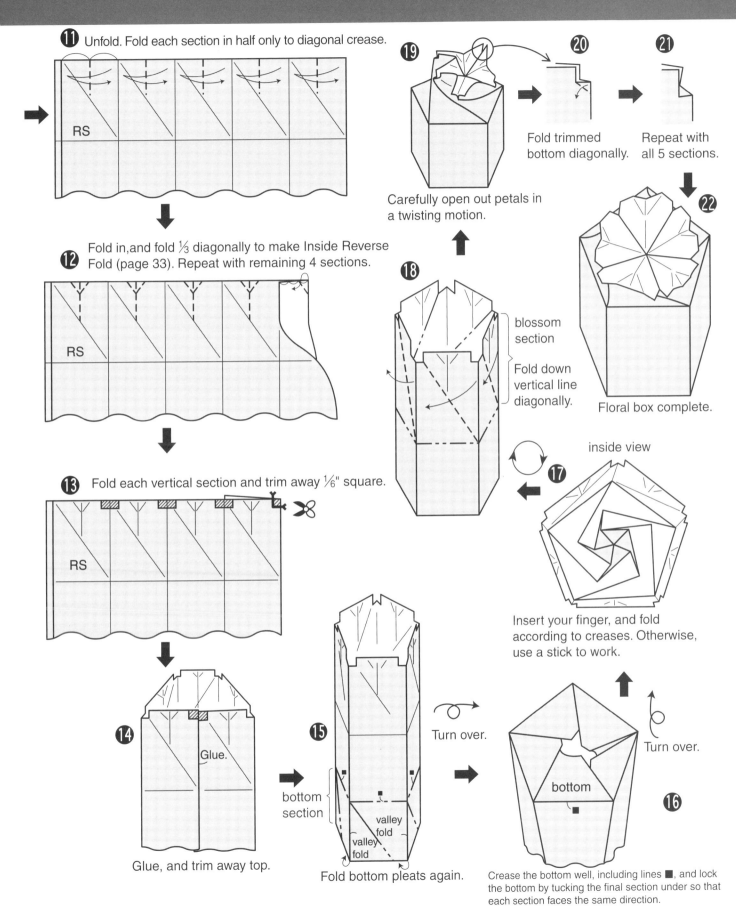

11 Unfold. Fold each section in half only to diagonal crease.

RS

12 Fold in, and fold ⅓ diagonally to make Inside Reverse Fold (page 33). Repeat with remaining 4 sections.

RS

13 Fold each vertical section and trim away ⅙" square.

RS

14 Glue.

Glue, and trim away top.

15 bottom section

valley fold

valley fold

Fold bottom pleats again.

Turn over.

16 bottom

Turn over.

Crease the bottom well, including lines ■, and lock the bottom by tucking the final section under so that each section faces the same direction.

17 inside view

Insert your finger, and fold according to creases. Otherwise, use a stick to work.

18 blossom section

Fold down vertical line diagonally.

Carefully open out petals in a twisting motion.

19

20 Fold trimmed bottom diagonally.

21 Repeat with all 5 sections.

22 Floral box complete.

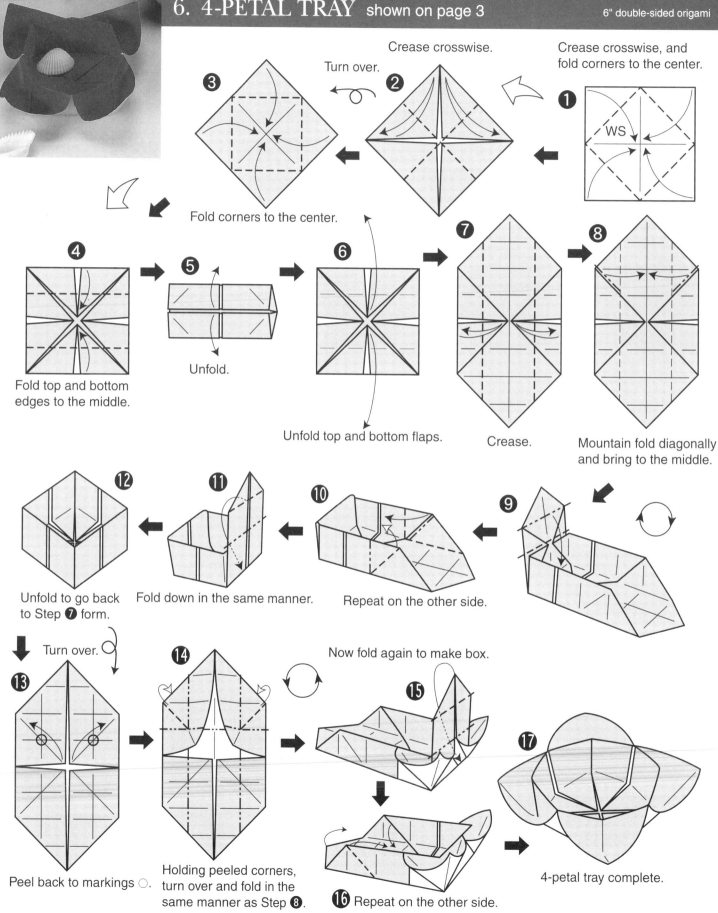

① Crease crosswise, and fold corners to the center.

WS

② Crease crosswise.

Turn over.

③ Fold corners to the center.

④ Fold top and bottom edges to the middle.

⑤ Unfold.

⑥ Unfold top and bottom flaps.

⑦ Crease.

⑧ Mountain fold diagonally and bring to the middle.

⑨

⑩ Repeat on the other side.

⑪ Fold down in the same manner.

⑫ Unfold to go back to Step ⑦ form.

Turn over.

⑬ Peel back to markings ○.

⑭ Holding peeled corners, turn over and fold in the same manner as Step ⑧.

⑮ Now fold again to make box.

⑯ Repeat on the other side.

⑰ 4-petal tray complete.

7. CHERRY BLOSSOMS shown on page 4

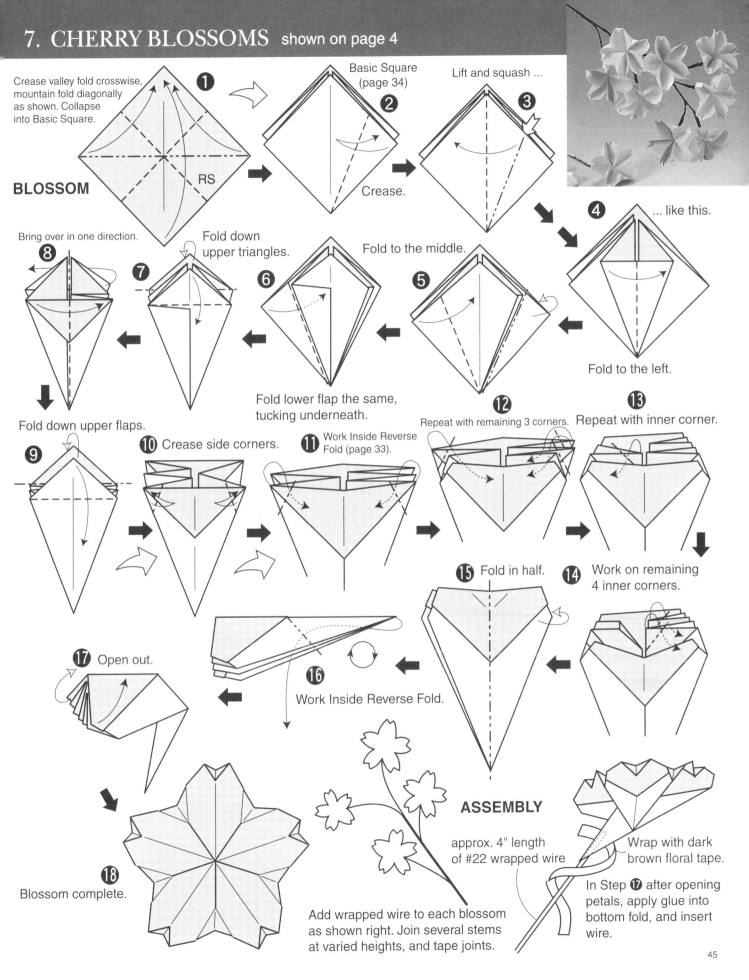

BLOSSOM

Crease valley fold crosswise, mountain fold diagonally as shown. Collapse into Basic Square.

❶

RS

❷ Basic Square (page 34)

Crease.

❸ Lift and squash ...

❹ ... like this.

Fold to the left.

❺ Fold to the middle.

❻ Fold down upper triangles.

Fold lower flap the same, tucking underneath.

❼

❽ Bring over in one direction.

Fold down upper flaps.

❾

❿ Crease side corners.

⓫ Work Inside Reverse Fold (page 33).

⓬ Repeat with remaining 3 corners.

⓭ Repeat with inner corner.

⓮ Work on remaining 4 inner corners.

⓯ Fold in half.

⓰ Work Inside Reverse Fold.

⓱ Open out.

⓲ Blossom complete.

ASSEMBLY

approx. 4" length of #22 wrapped wire

Add wrapped wire to each blossom as shown right. Join several stems at varied heights, and tape joints.

Wrap with dark brown floral tape.

In Step ⓱ after opening petals, apply glue into bottom fold, and insert wire.

45

8. DOGWOOD BLOSSOMS shown on page 5

BLOSSOM

1 RS

Crease valley fold crosswise, mountain fold diagonally as shown. Collapse into Basic Square.

2 Fold in trisection.

3 Bring over in one direction. Repeat behind.

4 Repeat with remaining 3 flaps.

5 Fold in diagonally leaving a trisection on upper side.

6 Bring over in one direction. Repeat behind.

Check that the corner reaches lower fold.

7 Repeat with remaining 3 flaps.

8 Unfold.

9 Insert finger and fold according to creases, diagonally and downwards.

10 Work on remaining 3 sections.

11

12 Blossom complete.

ASSEMBLY

Insert wired center of flower into center of blossom, and glue to secure.

Adjust center position to fit corners of blossom.

Wrap stem with dark brown floral tape.

Assemble stems varying heights. Tape down as you join single or double leaf stems.

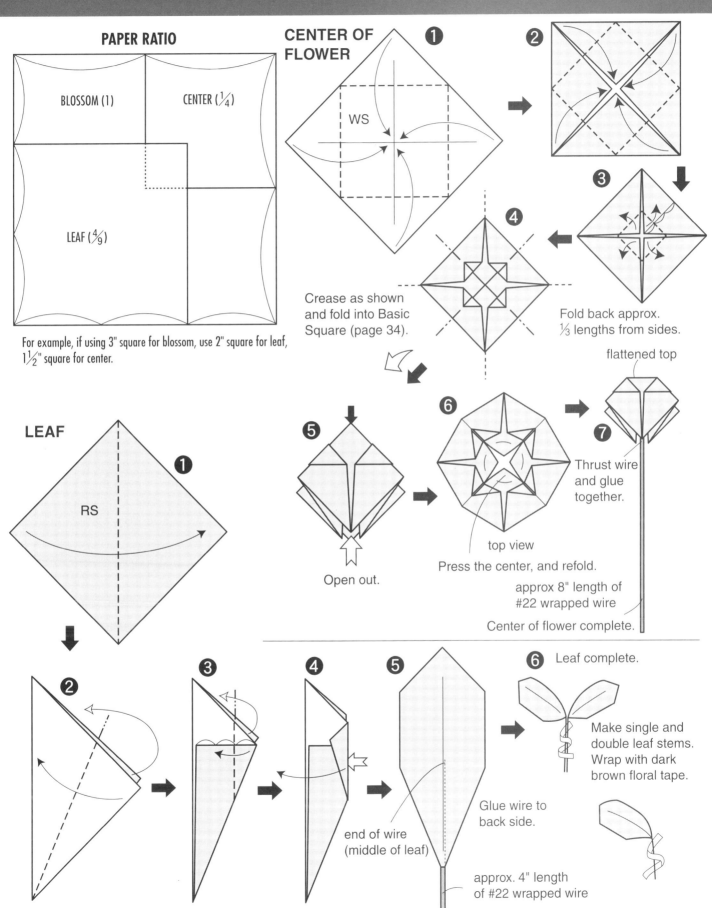

PAPER RATIO

BLOSSOM (1)

CENTER ($\frac{1}{4}$)

LEAF ($\frac{4}{9}$)

For example, if using 3" square for blossom, use 2" square for leaf, 1$\frac{1}{2}$" square for center.

CENTER OF FLOWER

❶ WS

❷

❸

❹ Crease as shown and fold into Basic Square (page 34).

Fold back approx. $\frac{1}{3}$ lengths from sides.

❺ Open out.

❻ top view

Press the center, and refold.

❼ flattened top

Thrust wire and glue together.

approx 8" length of #22 wrapped wire

Center of flower complete.

LEAF

❶ RS

❷

❸

❹ end of wire (middle of leaf)

❺ Glue wire to back side.

approx. 4" length of #22 wrapped wire

❻ Leaf complete.

Make single and double leaf stems. Wrap with dark brown floral tape.

10. VIOLET shown on page 7

FLOWER ❶

Make a Basic Pentagon beginning with right side up. Work to Step ⓳ of page 37.

PAPER RATIO

CALYX (1/9)

FLOWER/ LARGE LEAF (1)

SMALL LEAF (1/4)

2½"- 3" square piece of paper is recommended for flower.

❷ Fold a corner to the middle.

❸ Bring over, and repeat with remaining 4 corners.

Lift and squash.

❹

❺ Repeat behind.

❻ Bring one flap over.

Repeat Step ❺ with remaining 4 flaps.

❼

❽

Bring over, and repeat with remaining 4 flaps.

❾

Fold to the middle.

❿

Fold in half.

⓫

Divide folds into 2 and 3. Work Inside Reverse Fold.

⓬

⓭

Hold markings ● together, and open out petals.

⓮ Flower complete.

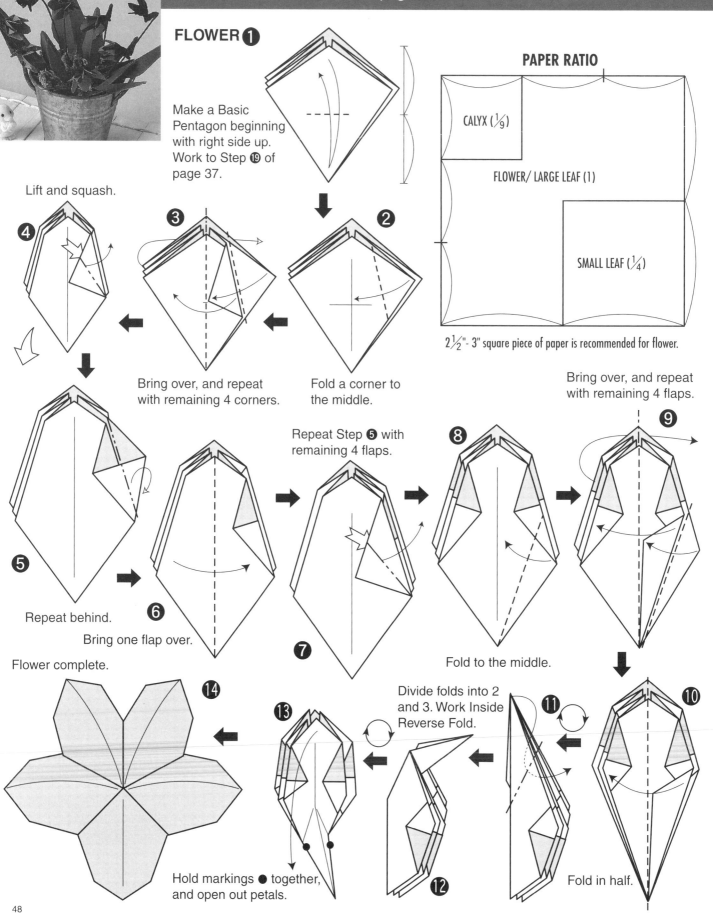

48

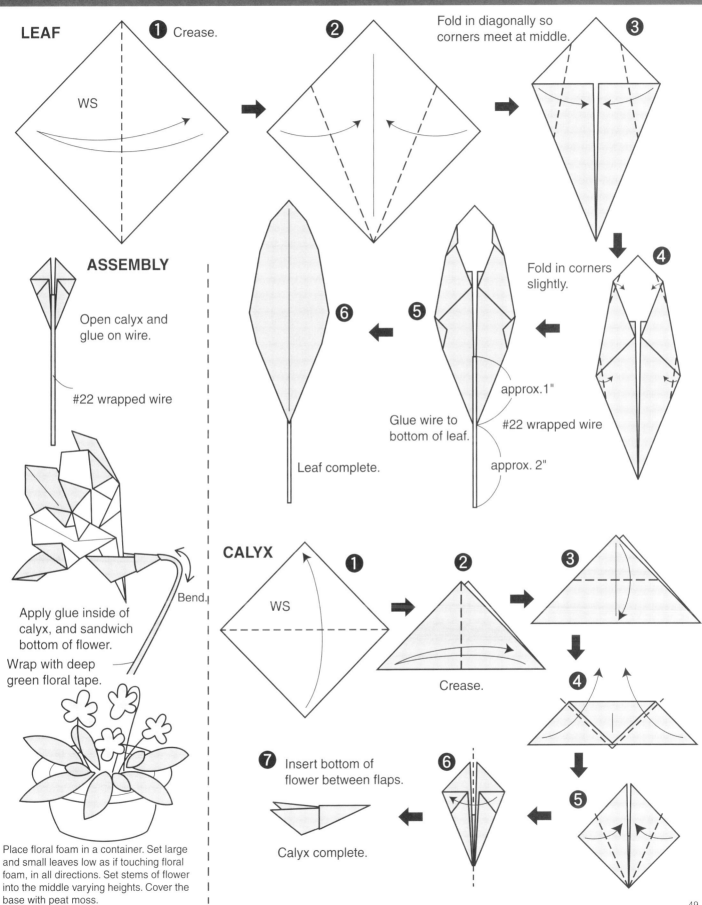

LEAF

① Crease.

WS

②

Fold in diagonally so corners meet at middle.

③

Fold in corners slightly.

④

⑥

Leaf complete.

⑤

Glue wire to bottom of leaf.

approx.1"

#22 wrapped wire

approx. 2"

ASSEMBLY

Open calyx and glue on wire.

#22 wrapped wire

Apply glue inside of calyx, and sandwich bottom of flower.

Wrap with deep green floral tape.

Bend.

Place floral foam in a container. Set large and small leaves low as if touching floral foam, in all directions. Set stems of flower into the middle varying heights. Cover the base with peat moss.

CALYX

①

WS

②

Crease.

③

④

⑤

⑥

⑦ Insert bottom of flower between flaps.

Calyx complete.

49

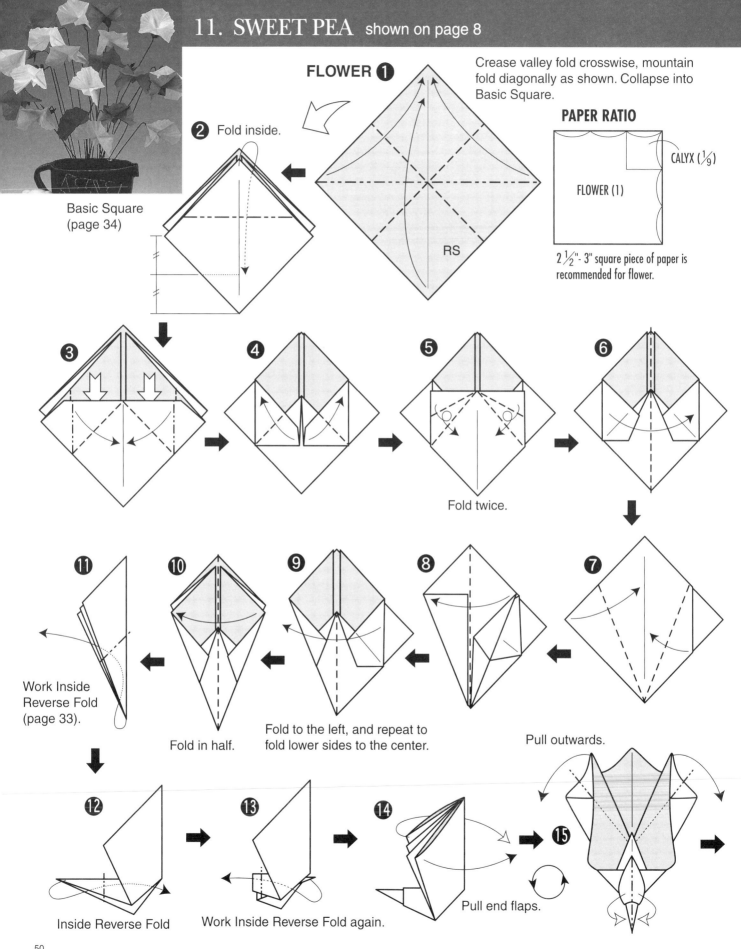

11. SWEET PEA shown on page 8

FLOWER ①

Crease valley fold crosswise, mountain fold diagonally as shown. Collapse into Basic Square.

PAPER RATIO

CALYX (1/9)

FLOWER (1)

2 1/2"- 3" square piece of paper is recommended for flower.

RS

② Fold inside.

Basic Square
(page 34)

③

④

⑤

Fold twice.

⑥

⑦

⑧

⑨

Fold to the left, and repeat to fold lower sides to the center.

⑩

Fold in half.

⑪

Work Inside Reverse Fold (page 33).

Pull outwards.

⑫

Inside Reverse Fold

⑬

Work Inside Reverse Fold again.

⑭

Pull end flaps.

⑮

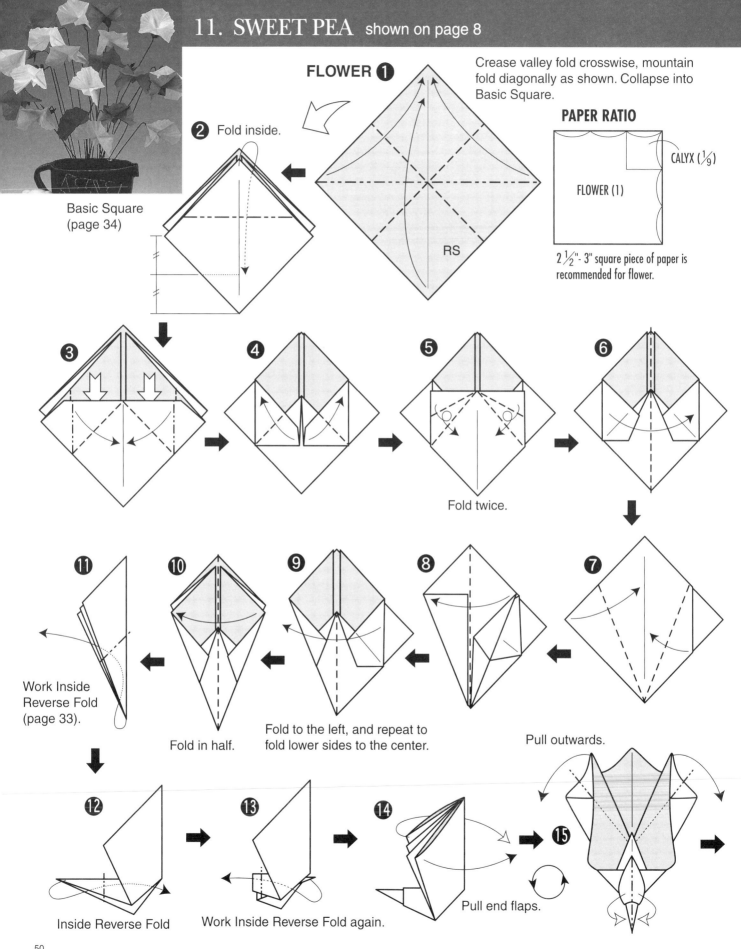

50

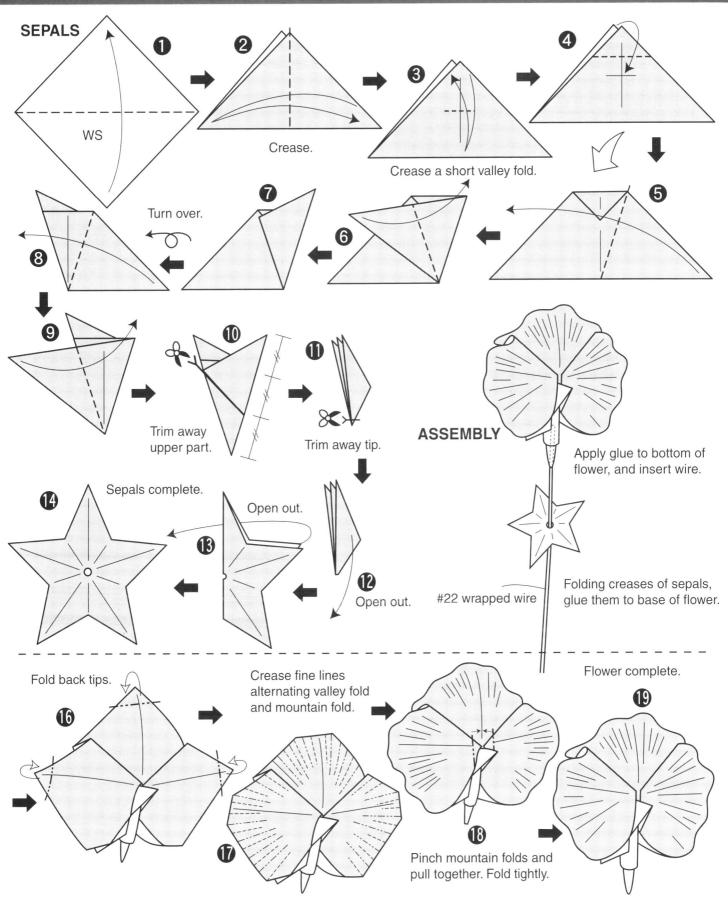

SEPALS

① WS

② Crease.

③ Crease a short valley fold.

④

⑤

⑥

⑦

Turn over.

⑧

⑨

⑩ Trim away upper part.

⑪ Trim away tip.

⑫ Open out.

⑬ Open out.

⑭ Sepals complete.

ASSEMBLY

Apply glue to bottom of flower, and insert wire.

#22 wrapped wire

Folding creases of sepals, glue them to base of flower.

⑯ Fold back tips.

⑰ Crease fine lines alternating valley fold and mountain fold.

⑱ Pinch mountain folds and pull together. Fold tightly.

⑲ Flower complete.

13. LILY OF THE VALLEY shown on page 10

FLORET

1 Make a short crease.

Suggested sizes and colors of paper
Floret: 2"-3" square white origami
Leaf: 6"-7" square green origami
Center: ⅔" square light green origami

Begin with a Basic Hexagon.
See page 35 and work only to Step **17**.

Crease by folding a corner to the middle and unfold.

2

Bring over. Repeat behind.

3

4

Repeat Steps **2** and **3** until all 6 flaps are creased.

5

Lift and push side fold inside to make Inside Reverse Fold (page 33). Repeat on the other side.

6 Work on remaining 5 folds. Apply glue as shown.

glue

7 Fold in only slightly in one direction.

8 Cut here.

Make a tiny crisscross cut for wire insertion.

Floret complete (upside down).

9

Using a stick or tweezers, round out into a bell shape.

CENTER OF FLOWER

Crease crosswise. Fold corners to the center.

1

WS

2

Make a Basic Square (page 34) by folding crosswise again.

Basic Square complete.

3 Bring over as shown. Repeat behind.

4 top view

Apply glue to end of wire, and insert into opening. Put together bottom tips and secure with glue.

5

approx. 2" #22 wrapped wire

6

Center of flower complete.

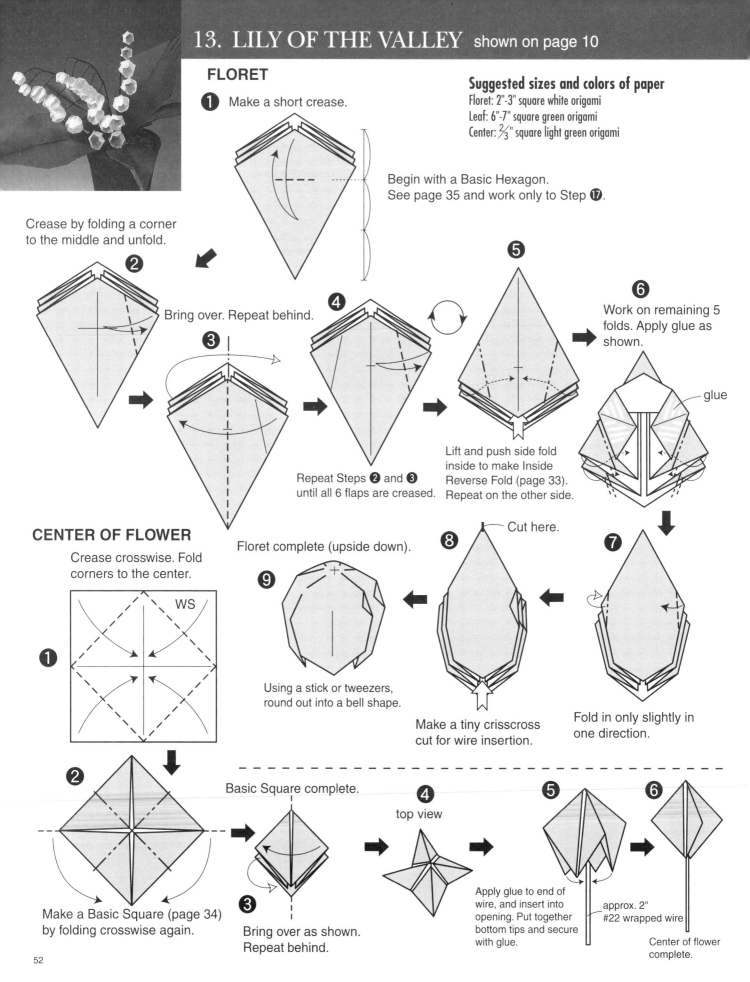

52

PAPER RATIO

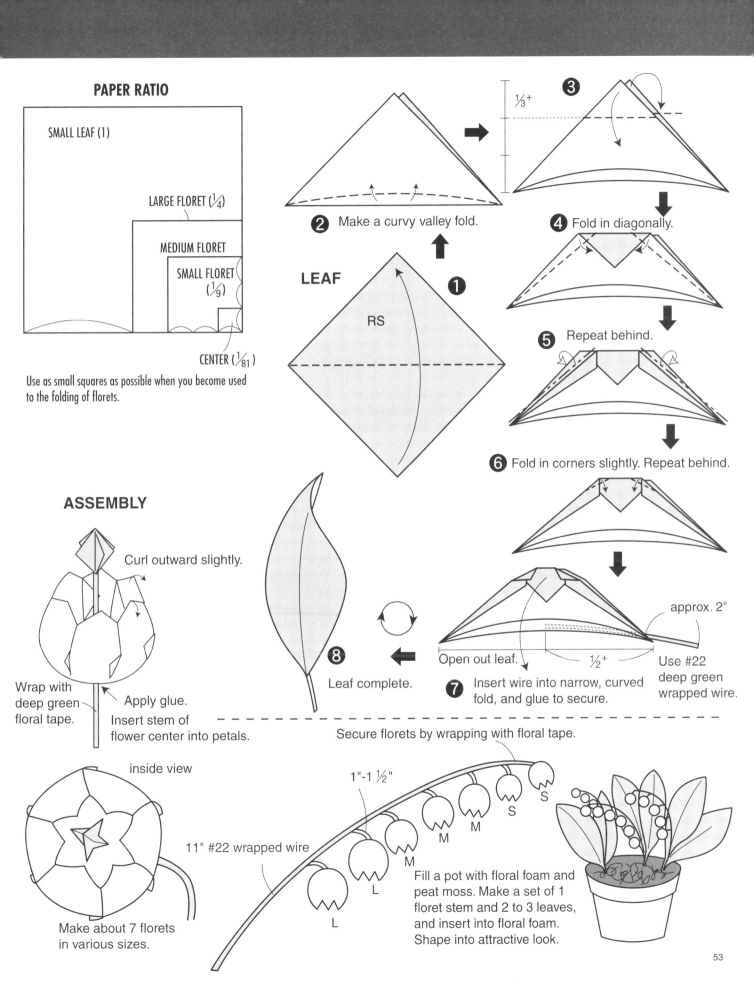

SMALL LEAF (1)

LARGE FLORET ($\frac{1}{4}$)

MEDIUM FLORET

SMALL FLORET ($\frac{1}{9}$)

CENTER ($\frac{1}{81}$)

Use as small squares as possible when you become used to the folding of florets.

LEAF

① RS

② Make a curvy valley fold.

③ $\frac{1}{3}^+$

④ Fold in diagonally.

⑤ Repeat behind.

⑥ Fold in corners slightly. Repeat behind.

approx. 2"

⑦ Insert wire into narrow, curved fold, and glue to secure.

Open out leaf. $\frac{1}{2}^+$ Use #22 deep green wrapped wire.

⑧ Leaf complete.

ASSEMBLY

Curl outward slightly.

Wrap with deep green floral tape.

Apply glue. Insert stem of flower center into petals.

Secure florets by wrapping with floral tape.

inside view

Make about 7 florets in various sizes.

11" #22 wrapped wire

1"-1 $\frac{1}{2}$"

L

L

M

M

M

S

S

Fill a pot with floral foam and peat moss. Make a set of 1 floret stem and 2 to 3 leaves, and insert into floral foam. Shape into attractive look.

53

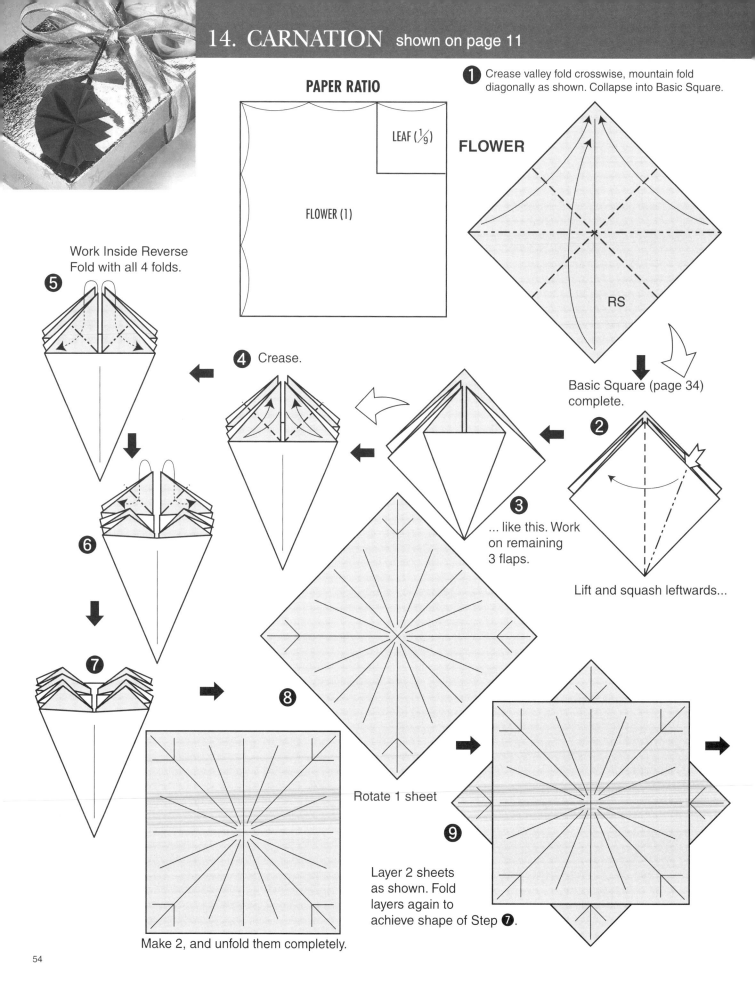

PAPER RATIO

LEAF (⅑)

FLOWER (1)

FLOWER

❶ Crease valley fold crosswise, mountain fold diagonally as shown. Collapse into Basic Square.

RS

Basic Square (page 34) complete.

❷

Lift and squash leftwards...

❸ ... like this. Work on remaining 3 flaps.

❹ Crease.

Work Inside Reverse Fold with all 4 folds.

❺

❻

❼

❽ Rotate 1 sheet

Make 2, and unfold them completely.

❾ Layer 2 sheets as shown. Fold layers again to achieve shape of Step ❼.

LEAF

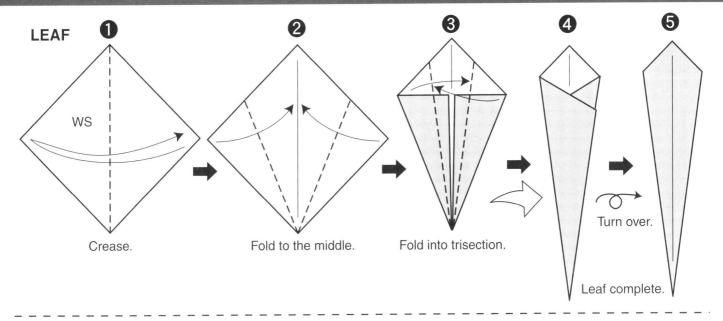

❶ Crease.

❷ Fold to the middle.

❸ Fold into trisection.

❹

❺ Turn over. Leaf complete.

WS

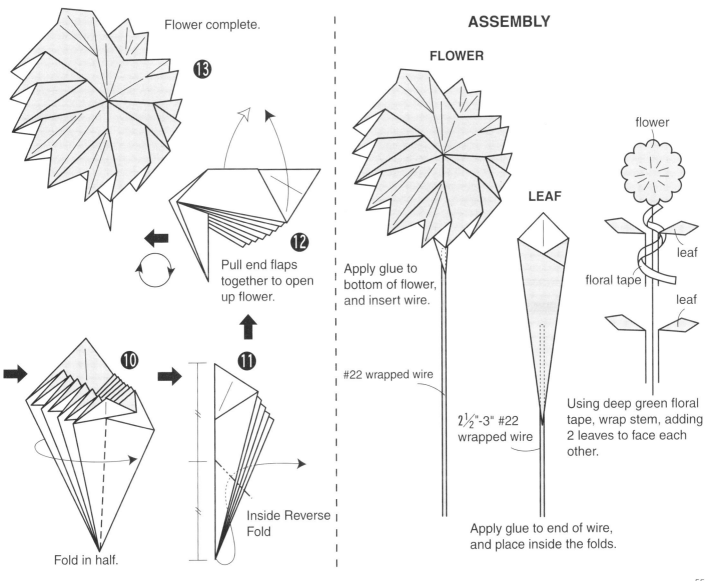

Flower complete.

❸

❷ Pull end flaps together to open up flower.

❿ Fold in half.

⓫ Inside Reverse Fold

ASSEMBLY

FLOWER

Apply glue to bottom of flower, and insert wire.

#22 wrapped wire

LEAF

$2\frac{1}{2}$"-3" #22 wrapped wire

Apply glue to end of wire, and place inside the folds.

flower

leaf

floral tape

leaf

Using deep green floral tape, wrap stem, adding 2 leaves to face each other.

15. ROSE shown on page 12

OUTER FLOWER

① Crease crosswise and unfold.
Fold corners to the center.

WS

PAPER RATIO

OUTER FLOWER (1)

INNER FLOWER/
LEAF ($\frac{1}{4}$)

② Fold corners to the center again...

③ ... like this.

Turn over.

④ Fold corners to the center...

⑤ ... like this.

Turn over.

Repeat.

⑥ Unfold and crease.

⑦

⑧ Pull outwards.

⑨ Crease inner flaps.

⑩ Repeat Steps **⑦** and **⑧**.

Outer Flower complete.

⑪ Set Inner Flower in the center for completion.

INNER FLOWER

See Steps ① and ② on opposite page. ➡

③

④

⑤ Set this into the center of Outer Flower.

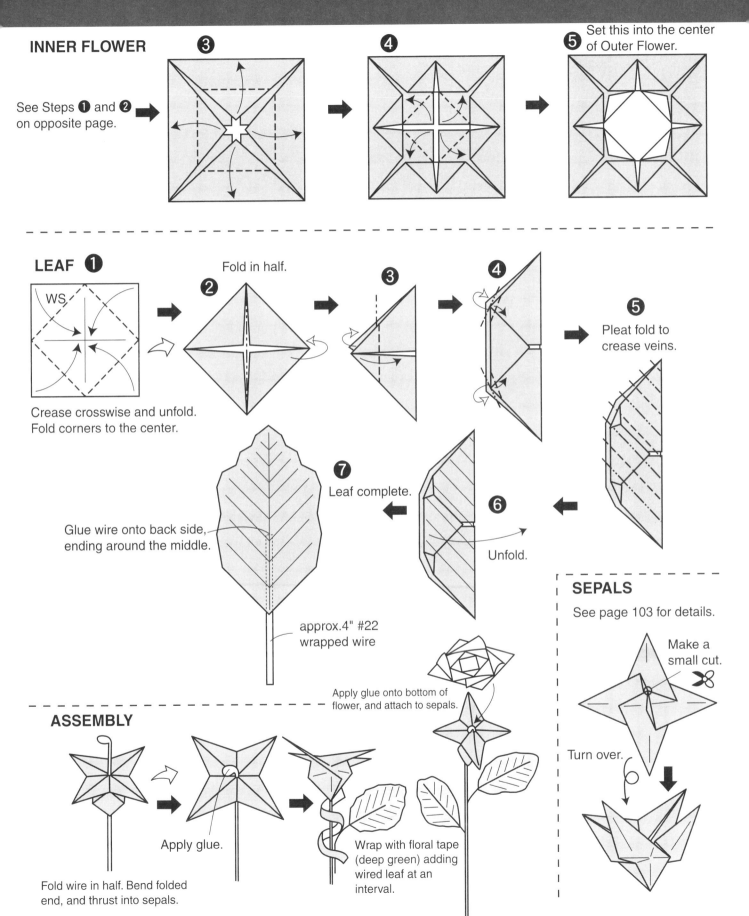

LEAF **①**

WS

Crease crosswise and unfold. Fold corners to the center.

② Fold in half.

③

④

⑤ Pleat fold to crease veins.

⑥ Unfold.

⑦ Leaf complete.

Glue wire onto back side, ending around the middle.

approx.4" #22 wrapped wire

SEPALS

See page 103 for details.

Make a small cut.

Turn over.

Apply glue onto bottom of flower, and attach to sepals.

ASSEMBLY

Apply glue.

Wrap with floral tape (deep green) adding wired leaf at an interval.

Fold wire in half. Bend folded end, and thrust into sepals.

16. CLIMBING ROSE shown on page 13

PAPER RATIO

FLOWER (1)

LEAF/ SEPAL (¼)

① Begin with Basic Square (page 34).

Crease and unfold.

② Refold center square as mountain fold. Reverse inner diagonal folds. Refold ...

③ ... like this. Fold left side to the center.

④ Bring folded flap over to right.

⑤ Repeat with remaining 3 sides.

⑥ Fold diagonally so that two dots meet.

⑦ Unfold.

⑧ Fold according to the arrows. Repeat behind.

⑨ Crease on remaining 3 sides. Be sure to crease well since these folds will raise the center.

⑩ Open out. Note the star position.

Turn over.

⑪ Pulling the star point towards you, open out circumference so that the center becomes 3D.

Press the center flat with your finger, and press the edges so that a rounded ridge is formed.

Turn over.

⑫ Crease.

⑬ Turn over. Crease.

⑭ Turn over. Pinch dotted folds, and fold according to the arrows, shaping a slight curve. Repeat with all dotted folds, one by one.

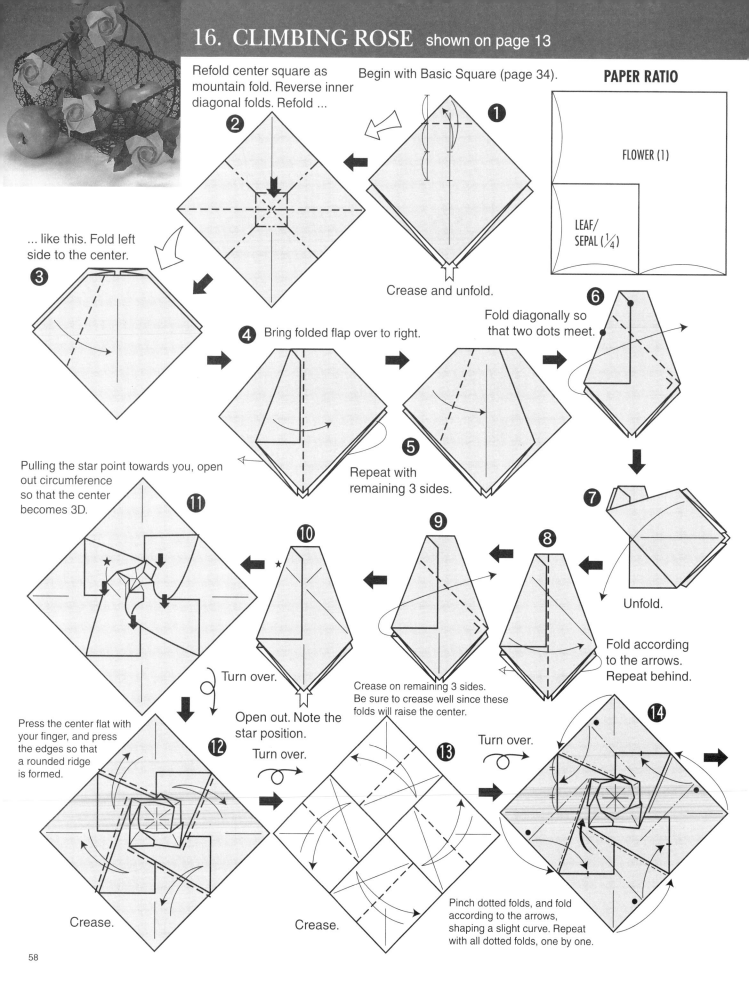

58

LEAF

WS

1 Crease.

2

3 Fold and pinch across the middle. Unfold.

4

5 Crease.

6 Fold down so that the crease made in Step **5** meets the bottom edge.

7 Fold to the middle.

Press down the triangles.

8

9 Make pleats by repeating Step-fold (page 33), and unfold.

10 Round off by folding in the corners.

Turn over.

11 Attach about 3" length of #22 wrapped wire with craft glue. Leaf complete.

SEPALS

See page 103 for instructions.

Sepals complete (a set of two).

ASSEMBLY

glue

#22 wrapped wire

Glue together.

glue

Wrap with deep green floral tape, occasionally adding leaves.

18 Flower complete.

17 Fold back lightly.

Turn over.

Fold in to secure the petals.

15 Fold in inner corners as you curve the outer petals.

Turn over.

16

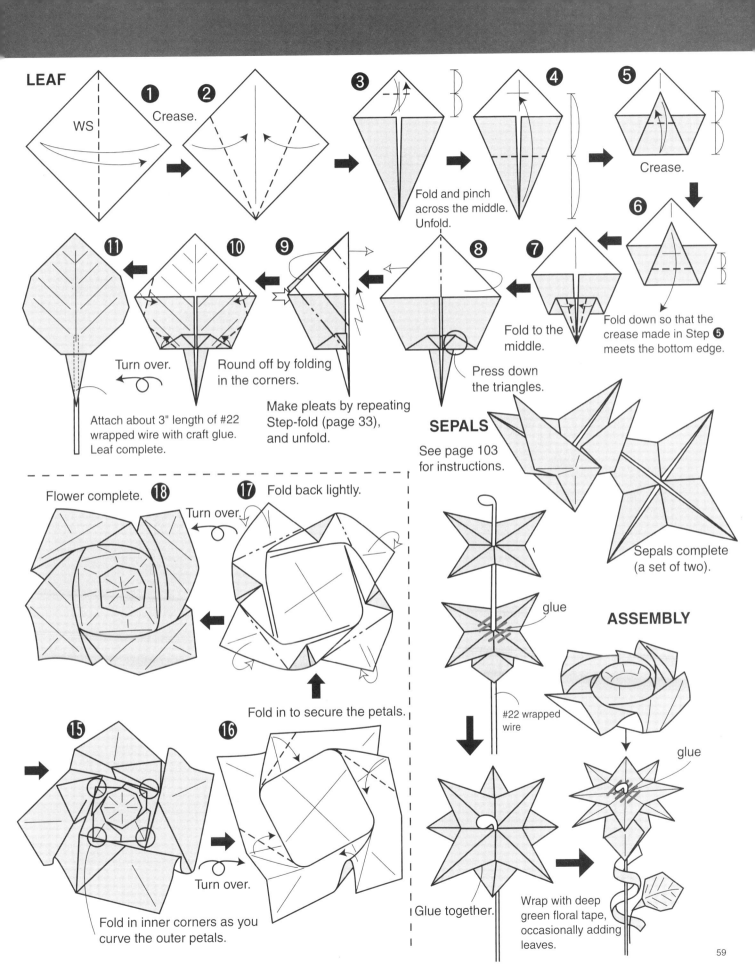

17. JAPANESE IRIS shown on page 14

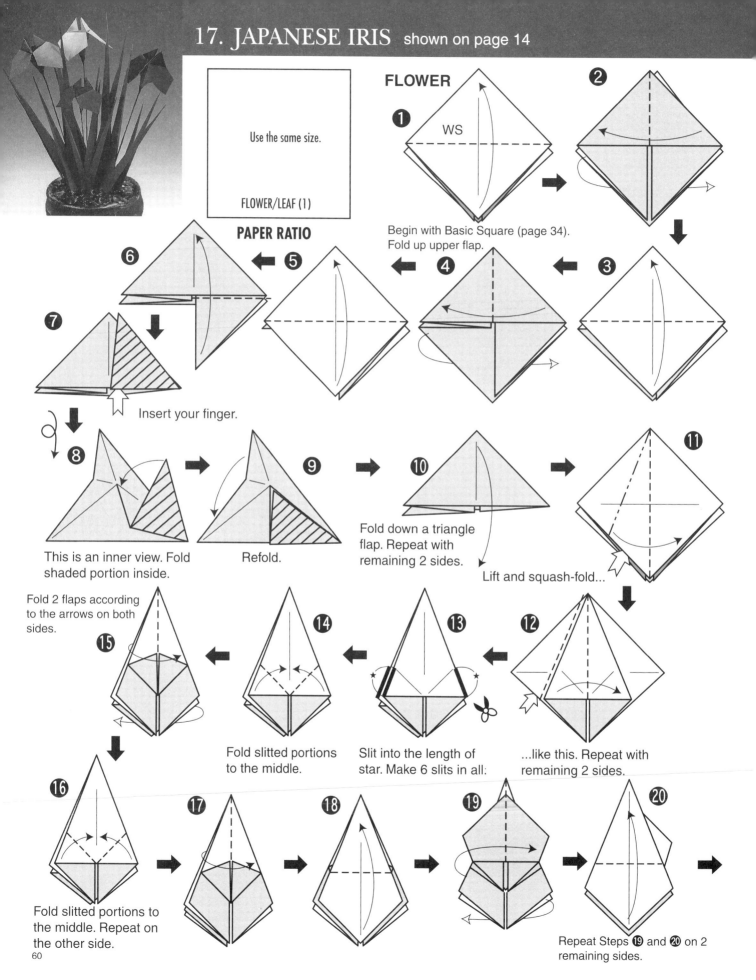

Use the same size.

FLOWER/LEAF (1)

PAPER RATIO

FLOWER

① WS

Begin with Basic Square (page 34). Fold up upper flap.

② ③ ④ ⑤

⑥ ⑦ Insert your finger.

⑧ This is an inner view. Fold shaded portion inside.

⑨ Refold.

⑩ Fold down a triangle flap. Repeat with remaining 2 sides.

⑪ Lift and squash-fold...

⑫ ...like this. Repeat with remaining 2 sides.

⑬ Slit into the length of star. Make 6 slits in all:

⑭ Fold slitted portions to the middle.

Fold 2 flaps according to the arrows on both sides.

⑮

⑯ Fold slitted portions to the middle. Repeat on the other side.

⑰ ⑱ ⑲ ⑳

Repeat Steps ⑲ and ⑳ on 2 remaining sides.

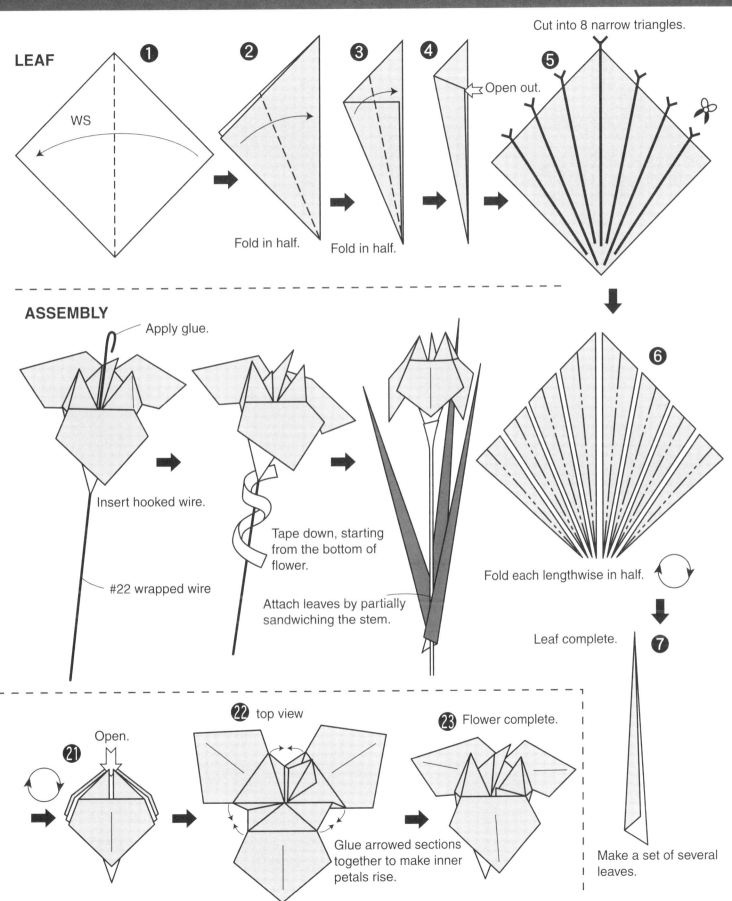

LEAF

① WS

② Fold in half.

③ Fold in half.

④ Open out.

⑤ Cut into 8 narrow triangles.

⑥ Fold each lengthwise in half.

Leaf complete.

⑦ Make a set of several leaves.

ASSEMBLY

Apply glue.

Insert hooked wire.

#22 wrapped wire

Tape down, starting from the bottom of flower.

Attach leaves by partially sandwiching the stem.

㉑ Open.

㉒ top view

Glue arrowed sections together to make inner petals rise.

㉓ Flower complete.

1

WS

Crease valley fold diagonally, and mountain fold crosswise as shown. Collapse into triangle.

2

Crease.

3

Fold up top layer, and squash-fold lifted center triangles ...

4

... like this. Fold down.

5

6

Allow space.

Fold up diagonally, into a 3D form. Press down lower section.

7

Repeat on the other side.

8

Lift upper portion, and fold the model in half ...

9

... like this. Fold under. Repeat behind.

10

Open out.

11

12

top view

Pinching the center tip, pull backwards and push into helmet.

13

Helmet complete.

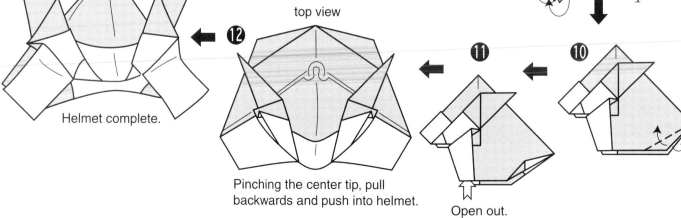

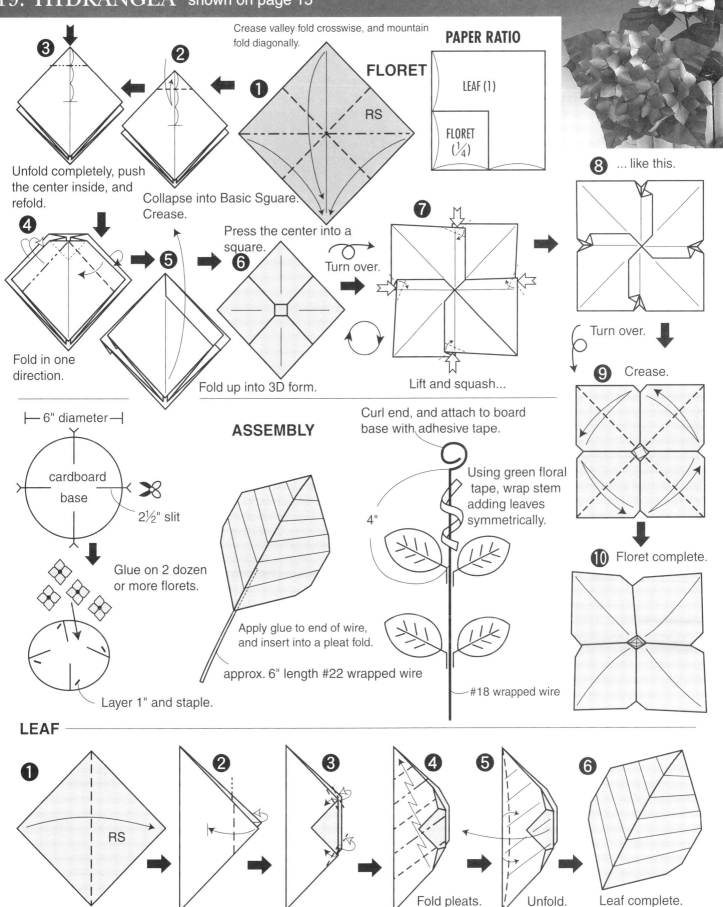

PAPER RATIO

FLORET

RS

Crease valley fold crosswise, and mountain fold diagonally.

❸ Unfold completely, push the center inside, and refold.

❷

❶ Collapse into Basic Square. Crease.

LEAF (1)

FLORET (¼)

❽ ... like this.

❹ Fold in one direction.

❺

❻ Press the center into a square.
Fold up into 3D form.

❼ Turn over.
Lift and squash...

Turn over.

❾ Crease.

❿ Floret complete.

ASSEMBLY

├─ 6" diameter ─┤

cardboard base

2½" slit

Glue on 2 dozen or more florets.

Layer 1" and staple.

Apply glue to end of wire, and insert into a pleat fold.

approx. 6" length #22 wrapped wire

Curl end, and attach to board base with adhesive tape.

4"

Using green floral tape, wrap stem adding leaves symmetrically.

#18 wrapped wire

LEAF

❶ RS

❷

❸

❹

❺

❻

Fold pleats.

Unfold.

Leaf complete.

FLOWER

❶ RS

Crease valley fold crosswise, and mountain fold diagonally. Collapse into Basic Square.

Basic Square

❷

Lift and squash leftwards...

❸ ... like this.
Fold to the right.

❹

❺ Turn over.

❻

❼

❽

❾

❿ Fold to the middle as shown.

⓫ Fold the length of star tightly. Repeat Step ❿ on remaining 4 sides.

End fold here. ★

⓬ Fold in along the colored edges.

⓭ Fold crease made in Steps ❿ to ⓬ into a curvy line. Repeat with remaining 4 folds.

⓮ Insert your finger, and press the fold securely.

⓯ Press the length of star tightly. Repeat with all sides.

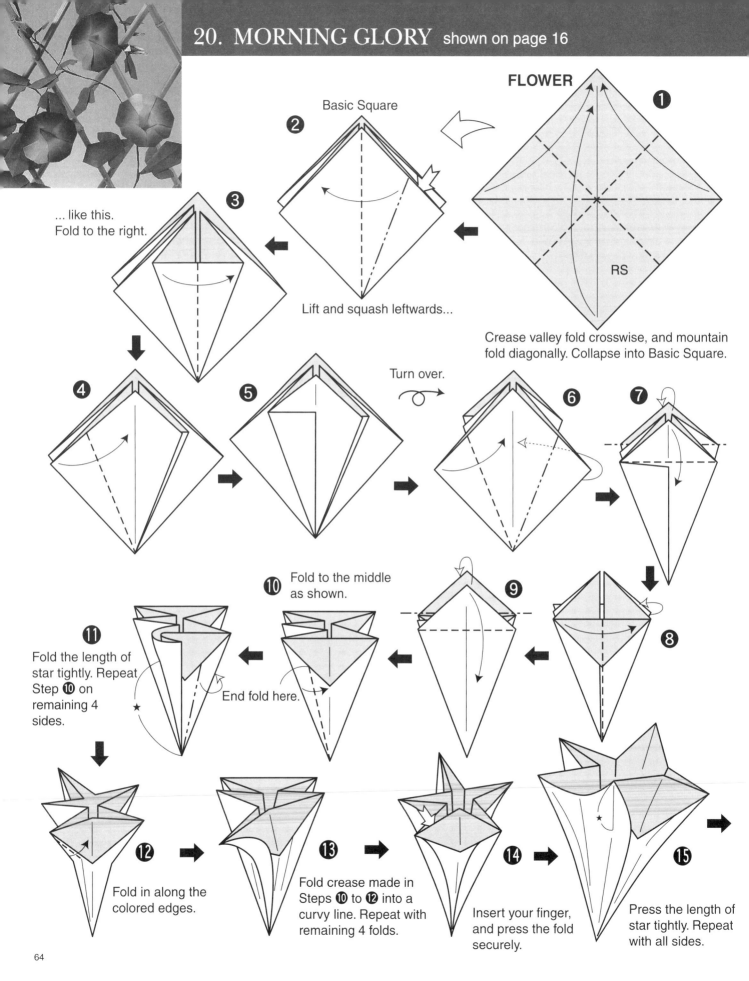

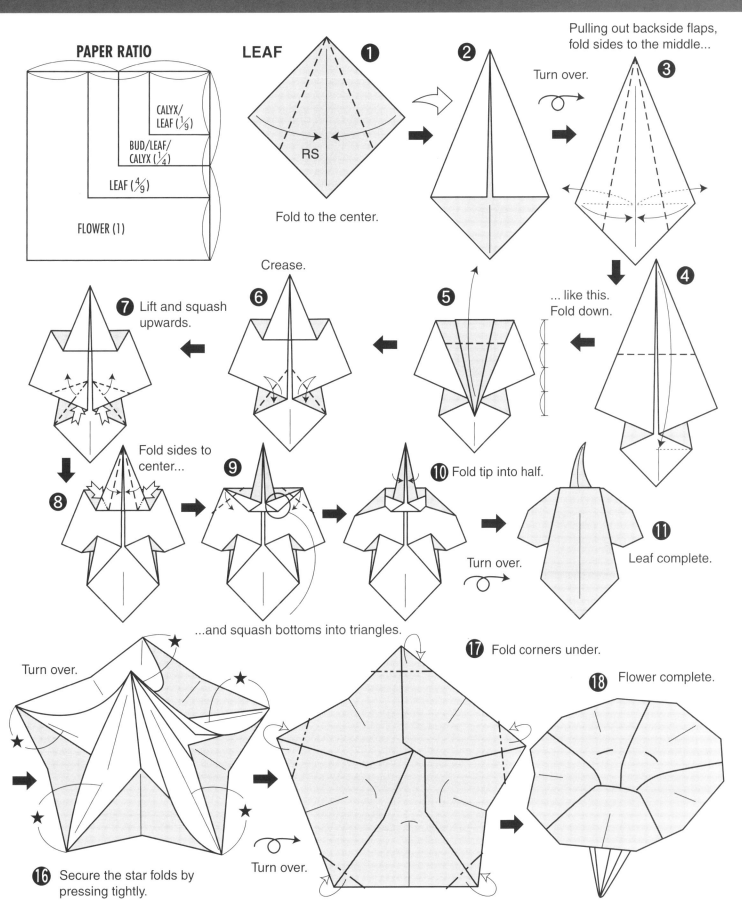

PAPER RATIO

CALYX/ LEAF (1/9)

BUD/LEAF/ CALYX (1/4)

LEAF (4/9)

FLOWER (1)

LEAF

1 Fold to the center.

RS

2 Turn over.

3 Pulling out backside flaps, fold sides to the middle...

4 ... like this. Fold down.

5

6 Crease.

7 Lift and squash upwards.

8 Fold sides to center...

9

10 Fold tip into half.

Turn over.

11 Leaf complete.

...and squash bottoms into triangles.

16 Secure the star folds by pressing tightly.

Turn over.

Turn over.

17 Fold corners under.

18 Flower complete.

65

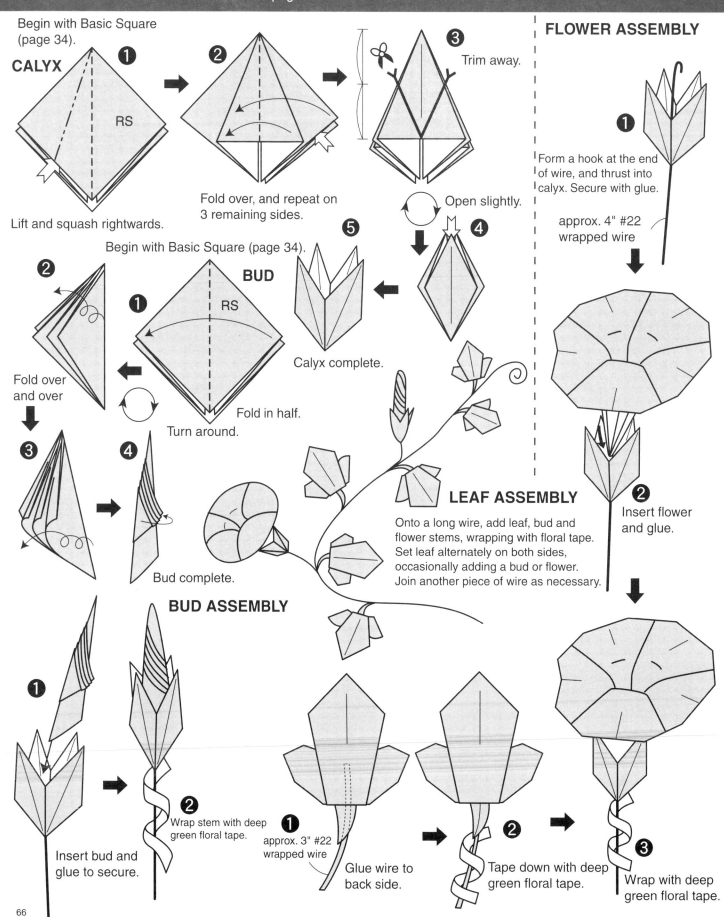

Begin with Basic Square (page 34).

CALYX

❶ RS

Lift and squash rightwards.

❷ Fold over, and repeat on 3 remaining sides.

❸ Trim away.

Open slightly.

❹

❺ Calyx complete.

Begin with Basic Square (page 34).

BUD

❶ RS

Fold in half.
Turn around.

❷

Fold over and over

❸

❹ Bud complete.

FLOWER ASSEMBLY

❶ Form a hook at the end of wire, and thrust into calyx. Secure with glue.

approx. 4" #22 wrapped wire

❷ Insert flower and glue.

LEAF ASSEMBLY

Onto a long wire, add leaf, bud and flower stems, wrapping with floral tape. Set leaf alternately on both sides, occasionally adding a bud or flower. Join another piece of wire as necessary.

BUD ASSEMBLY

❶

❷ Wrap stem with deep green floral tape.

Insert bud and glue to secure.

❶ approx. 3" #22 wrapped wire
Glue wire to back side.

❷ Tape down with deep green floral tape.

❸ Wrap with deep green floral tape.

9. PANSY shown on page 6

PAPER RATIO

FLOWER (1)

LEAF/ CENTER (¼)

FLOWER/ CENTER

1 Crease valley fold crosswise, and mountain fold diagonally. Collapse into Basic Square.

RS

2 Basic Square

3

4 Fold to the middle.

5

6

7

8 Repeat on the left side.

Make center of flower using a quarter size paper, and insert into flower.

9 center

flower

10 Fold in half.

11 Inside Reverse Fold

12 Bring sides together.

13 Flower complete.

ASSEMBLY

approx. 6" #22 wrapped wire

Glue wire onto back side of leaf.

Glue wire between folds, and secure with deep green floral tape.

Tape down.

LEAF

1 WS Fold to the middle.

2

3

4 Turn over. Leaf complete.

Place floral foam in a container, and cover it with peat moss. Set flowers and leaves in a balanced manner.

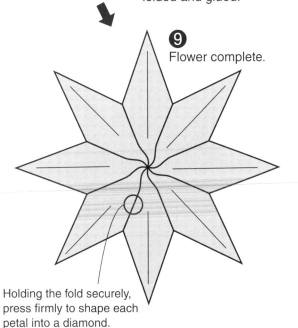

PAPER RATIO

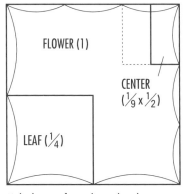

FLOWER (1)

CENTER (⅑ × ½)

LEAF (¼)

Make leaves of varied sizes by adjusting the size of paper.

Begin with Reverse Basic Octagon, Method 2 on page 36.

FLOWER

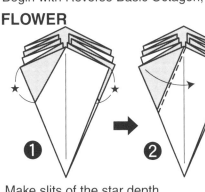

❶

❷ Make slits of the star depth into all 8 flaps.

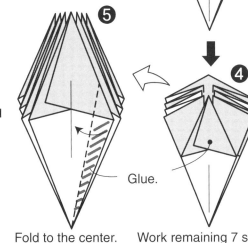

❸

❹ Work remaining 7 sides in the same manner.

Glue.

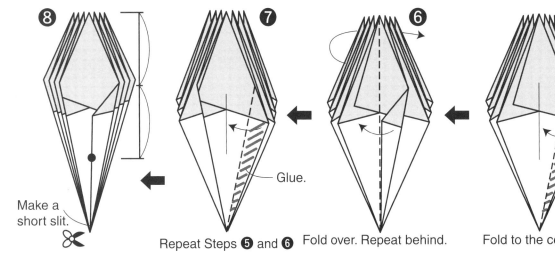

❺ Fold to the center.

Glue.

❻ Fold over. Repeat behind.

❼ Repeat Steps ❺ and ❻ until all 8 flaps are folded and glued.

Glue.

❽ Make a short slit.

❾ Flower complete.

Holding the fold securely, press firmly to shape each petal into a diamond.

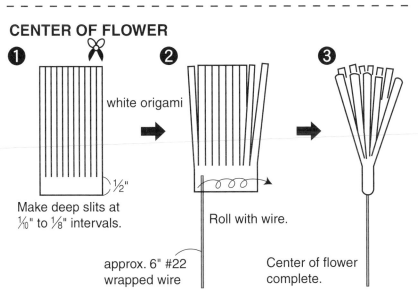

CENTER OF FLOWER

❶ Make deep slits at ⅒" to ⅛" intervals.

½"

❷ white origami

Roll with wire.

approx. 6" #22 wrapped wire

❸ Center of flower complete.

LEAF

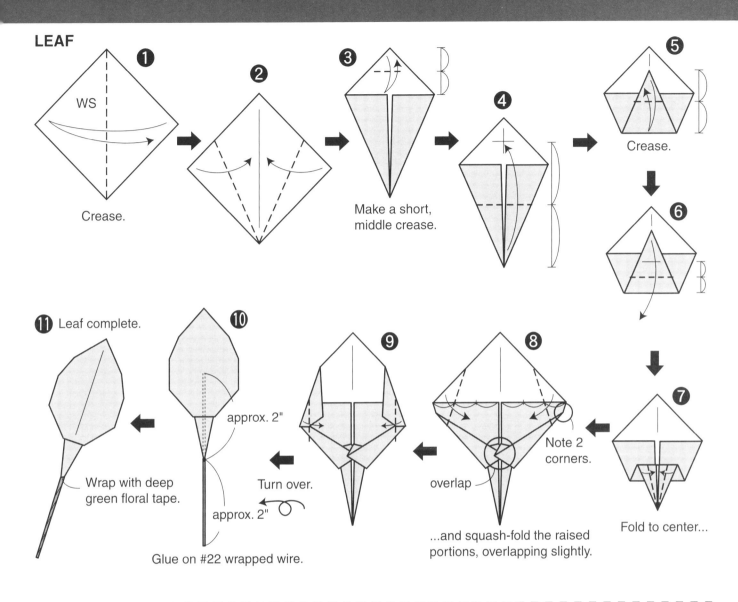

1 WS

Crease.

2

3 Make a short, middle crease.

4

5 Crease.

6

7 Fold to center...

8 Note 2 corners.

overlap

...and squash-fold the raised portions, overlapping slightly.

9

10 approx. 2"

approx. 2"

Glue on #22 wrapped wire.

Turn over.

11 Leaf complete.

Wrap with deep green floral tape.

ASSEMBLY

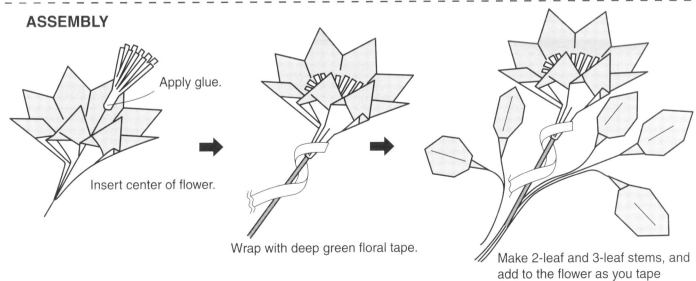

Apply glue.

Insert center of flower.

Wrap with deep green floral tape.

Make 2-leaf and 3-leaf stems, and add to the flower as you tape down. Shape into a vine.

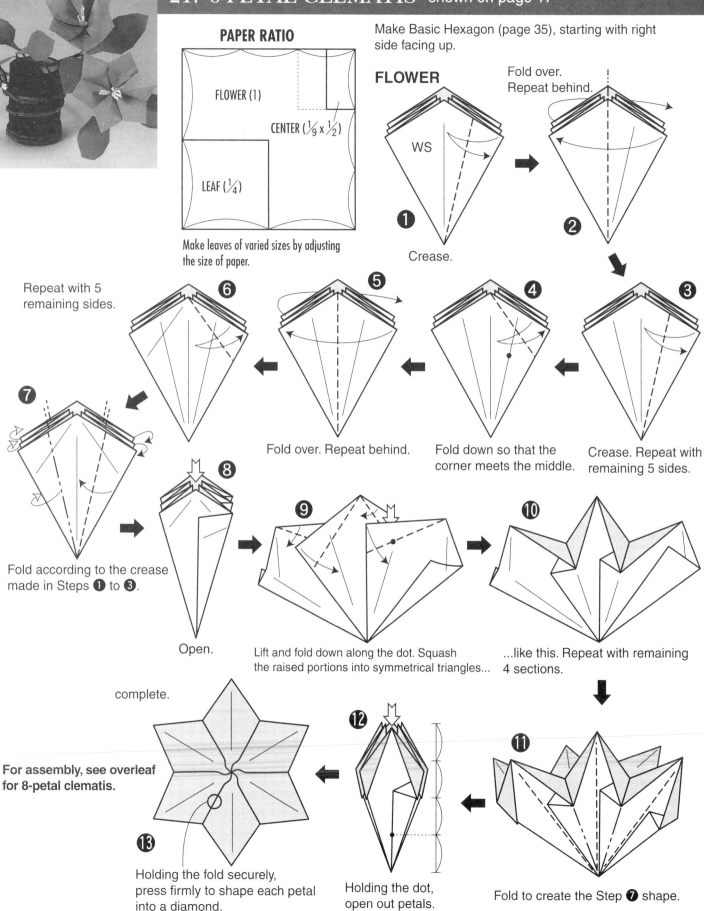

PAPER RATIO

FLOWER (1)

CENTER (1/9 x 1/2)

LEAF (1/4)

Make leaves of varied sizes by adjusting the size of paper.

Make Basic Hexagon (page 35), starting with right side facing up.

FLOWER

① WS

Crease.

② Fold over. Repeat behind.

③ Crease. Repeat with remaining 5 sides.

④ Fold down so that the corner meets the middle.

⑤ Fold over. Repeat behind.

⑥ Repeat with 5 remaining sides.

⑦ Fold according to the crease made in Steps ① to ③.

⑧ Open.

⑨ Lift and fold down along the dot. Squash the raised portions into symmetrical triangles...

⑩ ...like this. Repeat with remaining 4 sections.

⑪ Fold to create the Step ⑦ shape.

⑫ Holding the dot, open out petals.

⑬ complete.

Holding the fold securely, press firmly to shape each petal into a diamond.

For assembly, see overleaf for 8-petal clematis.

FLOWER

❶ WS

Crease valley fold crosswise, and mountain fold diagonally as shown. Collapse into Basic Square.

❷ Basic Square

❸ Tuck triangle under.

❹

❺ Repeat with remaining 2 sides.

❻ Fold the triangles in half. Repeat with remaining 2 sides.

❼ Unfold.

❽ Push the creased portion inside to form Inside Reverse Fold (page 33). Repeat with 2 remaining sides.

❾ Fold the inner triangle in half.

❿ Repeat with remaining 2 inner triangles.

⓫ Pull to make 3D shape.

⓬ Flower complete.

LEAF

Fold to diagonal center.

❶ WS

❷ Fold to middle.

❸ Fold to middle again.

❹ Turn over.

❺ Leaf complete.

FLOWER

LEAF

ASSEMBLY

Using deep green floral tape, tape down the wire. Add leaf stems and tape together.

approx. 8" #22 wrapped wire

Bend end of wire and insert into flower. Glue.

Apply glue to wire, and attach inside.

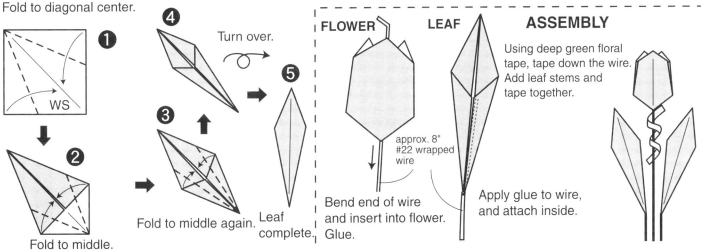

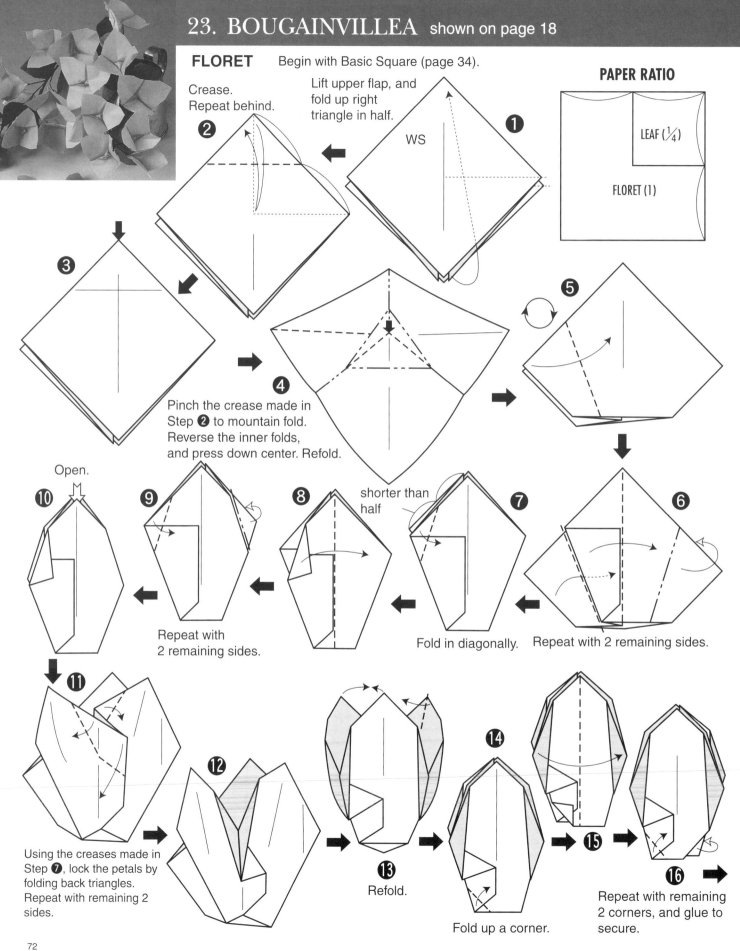

FLORET Begin with Basic Square (page 34).

1 Lift upper flap, and fold up right triangle in half. WS

2 Crease. Repeat behind.

3

4 Pinch the crease made in Step **2** to mountain fold. Reverse the inner folds, and press down center. Refold.

5

6 Repeat with 2 remaining sides.

7 shorter than half

8 Fold in diagonally.

9 Repeat with 2 remaining sides.

10 Open.

11 Using the creases made in Step **7**, lock the petals by folding back triangles. Repeat with remaining 2 sides.

12

13 Refold.

14 Fold up a corner.

15

16 Repeat with remaining 2 corners, and glue to secure.

PAPER RATIO

LEAF (¼)

FLORET (1)

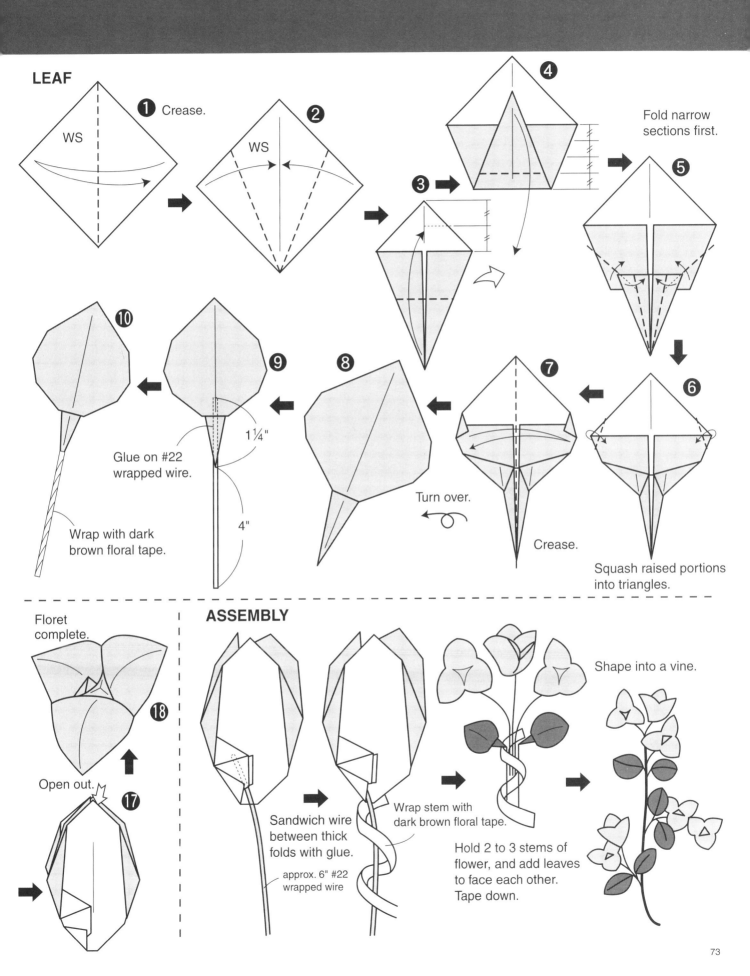

LEAF

❶ Crease. WS

❷ WS

❸

❹ Fold narrow sections first.

❺

❻

❼ Crease.

Squash raised portions into triangles.

Turn over.

❽

❾ 1¼" 4"

❿ Glue on #22 wrapped wire.

Wrap with dark brown floral tape.

Floret complete.

⓲

Open out.

⓱

ASSEMBLY

Sandwich wire between thick folds with glue.

approx. 6" #22 wrapped wire

Wrap stem with dark brown floral tape.

Hold 2 to 3 stems of flower, and add leaves to face each other. Tape down.

Shape into a vine.

FLOWER

PAPER RATIO

	LEAF/CENTER ($\frac{1}{4}$)
FLOWER (1)	

Vary the size of leaves by slightly enlarging or lessening the above ratio.

① WS

Crease valley fold crosswise, and mountain fold diagonally as shown. Collapse into Basic Square.

Basic Square (page 34)

② Lift and squash-fold rightwards. Fold over and repeat.

③

④ Fold to the middle.

⑤ Turn over.

⑥ Repeat Steps **②** to **⑤**.

⑦

⑧ Fold over. Repeat behind.

⑨

⑩ Open out.

⑪ Reverse the folds and refold.

⑫ Make slits of the star length into 6 folds.

⑬

⑭

⑮ Repeat with remaining 5 sides.

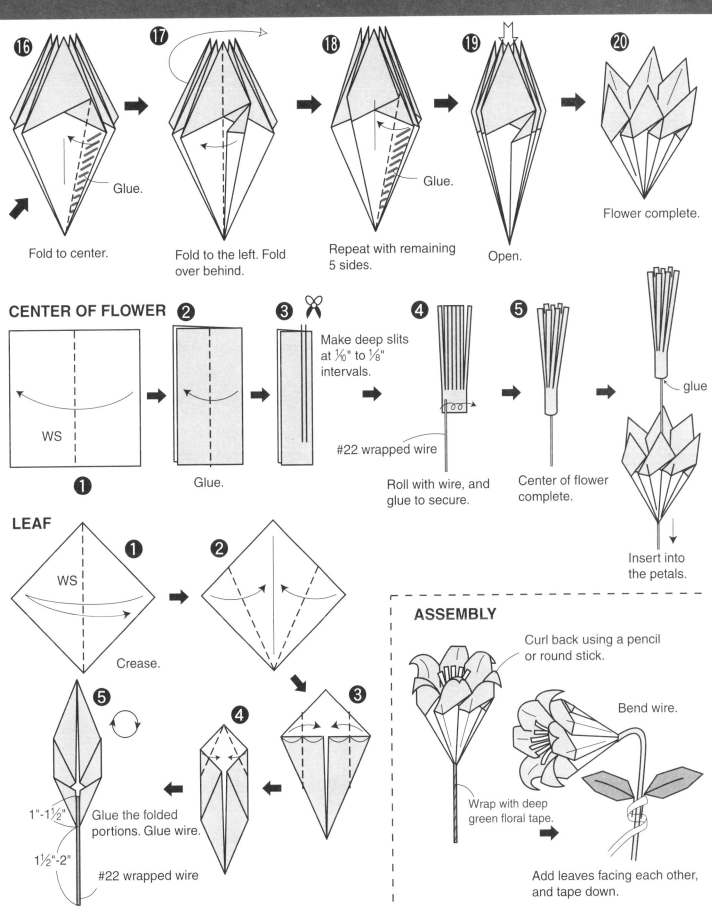

16 Fold to center. Glue.

17 Fold to the left. Fold over behind.

18 Repeat with remaining 5 sides. Glue.

19 Open.

20 Flower complete.

CENTER OF FLOWER

1 WS

2 Glue.

3 Make deep slits at $\frac{1}{10}$" to $\frac{1}{8}$" intervals.

4 #22 wrapped wire
Roll with wire, and glue to secure.

5 Center of flower complete.

glue

Insert into the petals.

LEAF

1 WS
Crease.

2

3

4

5 Glue the folded portions. Glue wire.
1"-1½"
1½"-2"
#22 wrapped wire
Leaf complete.

ASSEMBLY

Curl back using a pencil or round stick.

Bend wire.

Wrap with deep green floral tape.

Add leaves facing each other, and tape down.

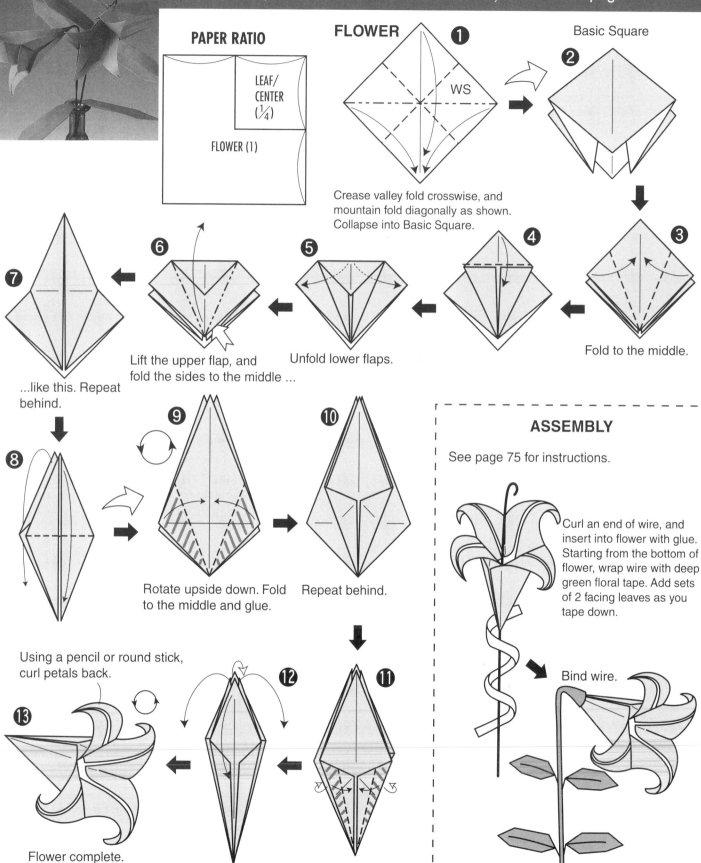

PAPER RATIO

LEAF/CENTER (¼)

FLOWER (1)

FLOWER

❶ Basic Square

❷

Crease valley fold crosswise, and mountain fold diagonally as shown. Collapse into Basic Square.

❸ Fold to the middle.

❹

❺ Unfold lower flaps.

❻ Lift the upper flap, and fold the sides to the middle ...

❼ ...like this. Repeat behind.

❽

❾ Rotate upside down. Fold to the middle and glue.

❿ Repeat behind.

⓫ Fold again to the middle. Repeat behind.

⓬ Pull down petals.

⓭ Flower complete.

Using a pencil or round stick, curl petals back.

ASSEMBLY

See page 75 for instructions.

Curl an end of wire, and insert into flower with glue. Starting from the bottom of flower, wrap wire with deep green floral tape. Add sets of 2 facing leaves as you tape down.

Bind wire.

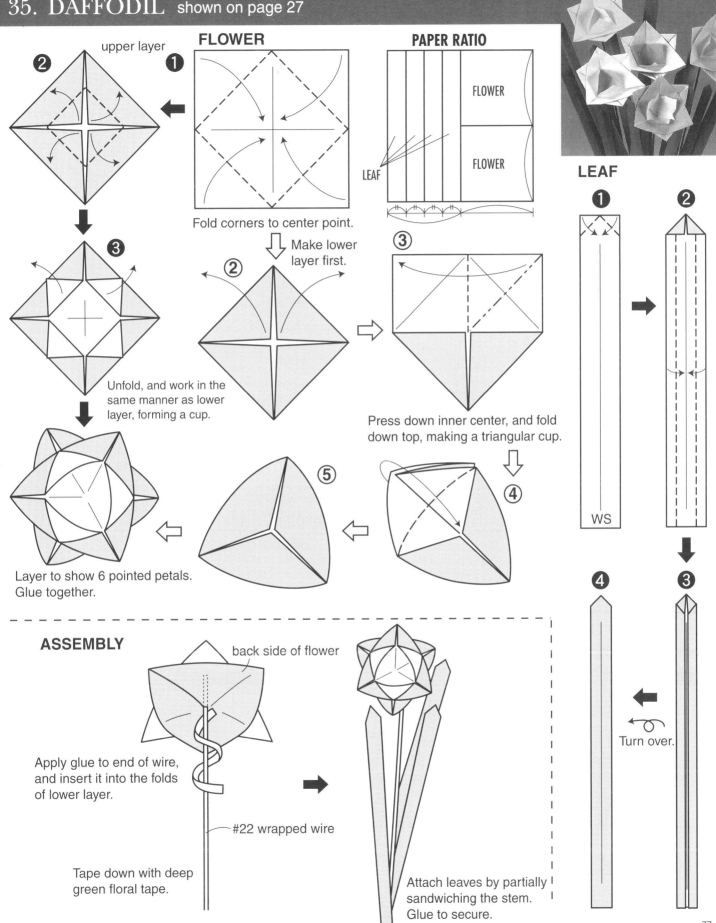

FLOWER

1 Fold corners to center point.

2 upper layer

Make lower layer first.

PAPER RATIO

LEAF

FLOWER

FLOWER

2

3 Unfold, and work in the same manner as lower layer, forming a cup.

3 Press down inner center, and fold down top, making a triangular cup.

4

5

Layer to show 6 pointed petals. Glue together.

LEAF

1

2

WS

4   **3**

Turn over.

ASSEMBLY

back side of flower

Apply glue to end of wire, and insert it into the folds of lower layer.

#22 wrapped wire

Tape down with deep green floral tape.

Attach leaves by partially sandwiching the stem. Glue to secure.

77

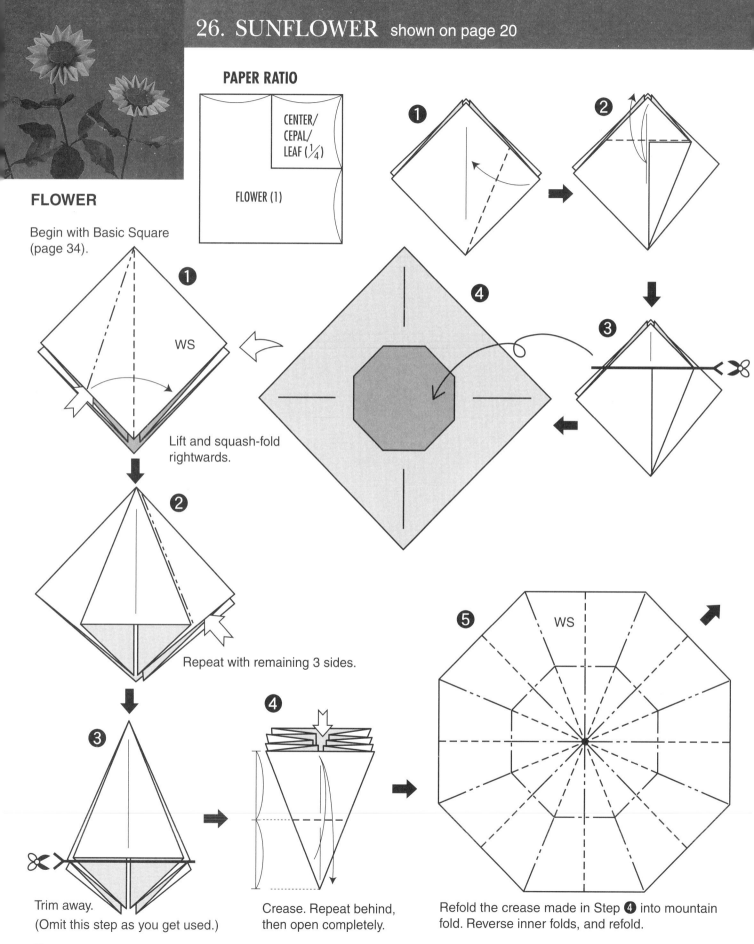

PAPER RATIO

CENTER/
CEPAL/
LEAF (¼)

FLOWER (1)

FLOWER

Begin with Basic Square
(page 34).

❶

WS

Lift and squash-fold
rightwards.

❷

Repeat with remaining 3 sides.

❸

Trim away.
(Omit this step as you get used.)

❹

Crease. Repeat behind,
then open completely.

❺

WS

Refold the crease made in Step ❹ into mountain
fold. Reverse inner folds, and refold.

❶

❷

❸

❹

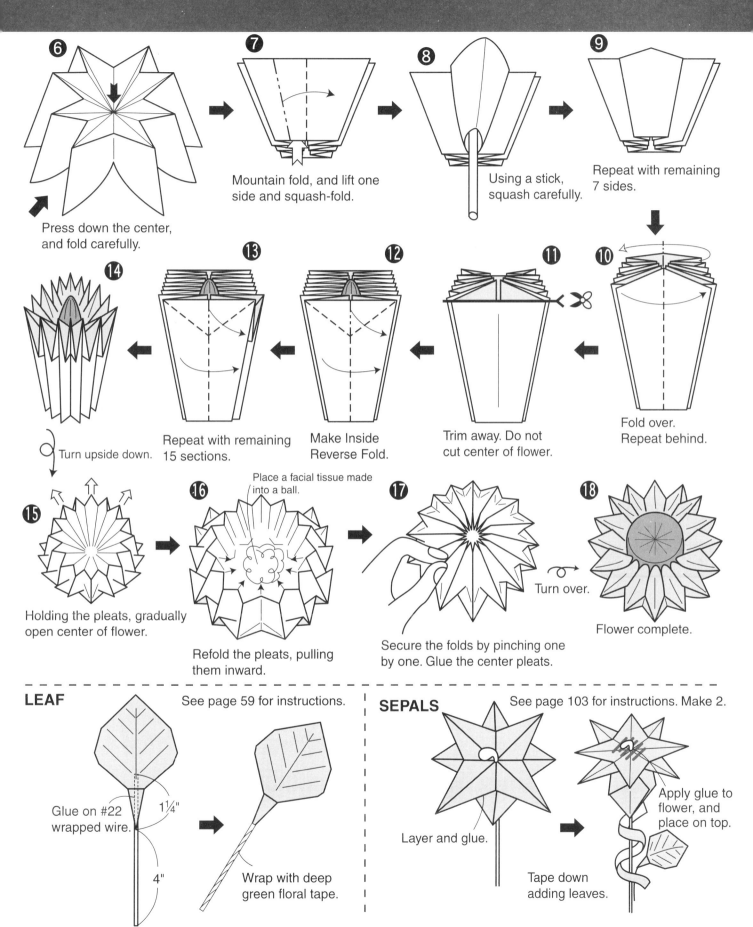

⑥ Press down the center, and fold carefully.

⑦ Mountain fold, and lift one side and squash-fold.

⑧ Using a stick, squash carefully.

⑨ Repeat with remaining 7 sides.

⑩ Fold over. Repeat behind.

⑪ Trim away. Do not cut center of flower.

⑫ Make Inside Reverse Fold.

⑬ Repeat with remaining 15 sections.

⑭ Turn upside down.

⑮ Holding the pleats, gradually open center of flower.

⑯ Place a facial tissue made into a ball. Refold the pleats, pulling them inward.

⑰ Secure the folds by pinching one by one. Glue the center pleats.

⑱ Turn over. Flower complete.

LEAF See page 59 for instructions.

Glue on #22 wrapped wire. 1¼" 4"

Wrap with deep green floral tape.

SEPALS See page 103 for instructions. Make 2.

Layer and glue.

Apply glue to flower, and place on top.

Tape down adding leaves.

FLOWER
Begin with Basic Square (page 34).

PAPER RATIO

LEAF 3"
INNER PETAL 3½"
MIDDLE PETAL 5"
BOTTOM PETAL 6"

❶ WS

Lift and squash-fold leftwards.

❷ Fold to one direction. Repeat behind.

❸ Repeat Steps ❶ and ❷ with remaining 3 sides.

❹ Fold over. Repeat behind.

❺

❻ Repeat with remaining 3 sides.

❼ Fold in half.

❽

❾ Inside Reverse Fold

❿

Turn over.

⓫ Pulling points ● together, crease 3D diagonals. Repeat with remaining 7 sections.

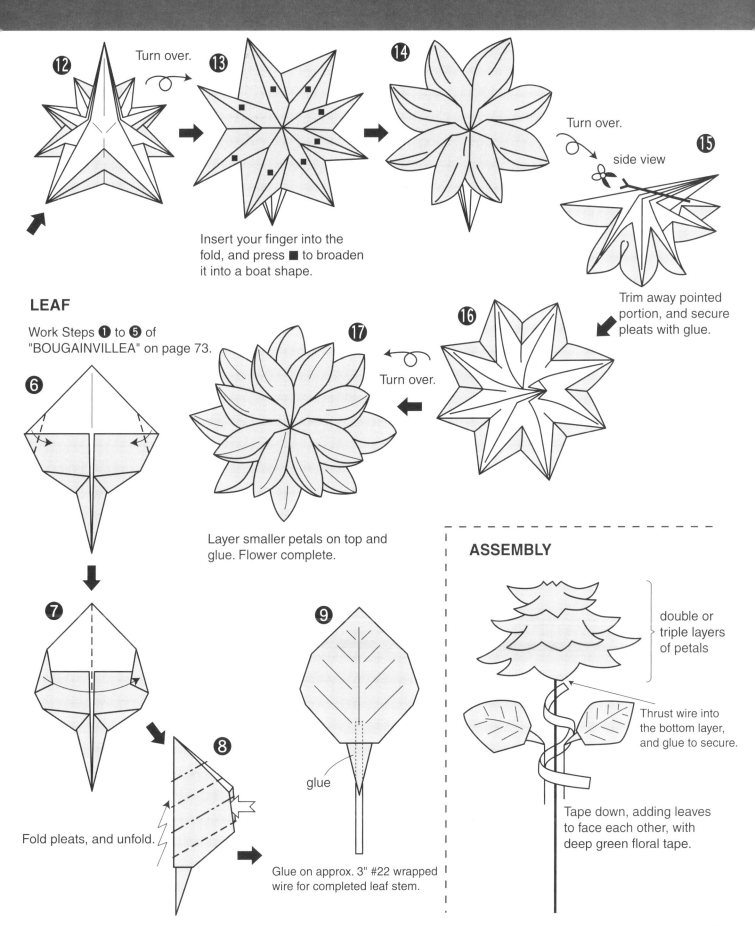

12 Turn over. **13**

14

Turn over.

side view **15**

Insert your finger into the fold, and press ■ to broaden it into a boat shape.

Trim away pointed portion, and secure pleats with glue.

LEAF

Work Steps **1** to **5** of "BOUGAINVILLEA" on page 73.

16

17 Turn over.

6

Layer smaller petals on top and glue. Flower complete.

7

9

ASSEMBLY

double or triple layers of petals

Thrust wire into the bottom layer, and glue to secure.

8

glue

Fold pleats, and unfold.

Glue on approx. 3" #22 wrapped wire for completed leaf stem.

Tape down, adding leaves to face each other, with deep green floral tape.

FLORET Begin with Basic Square (page 34).

PAPER RATIO

CENTER/ CALYX (1/4)

LEAF (4/9)

FLORET(1)

RS

1

2

3

Fold over. Repeat behind.

4

Repeat with remaining 3 sides.

5

Unfold...

6

...to this shape. Make Inside Reverse Fold.

7

Lift and fold back to lock the inner triangle.

Repeat with remaining 4 sides.

8

Turn upside down.

9

Fold according to the creases.

10

Fold diagonally.

11

Repeat with remaining 3 sides.

12

Insert your finger.

13

Floret complete.

CENTER OF FLOWER   Begin with Basic Square (page 34).

For ASSEMBLY, see page 84.

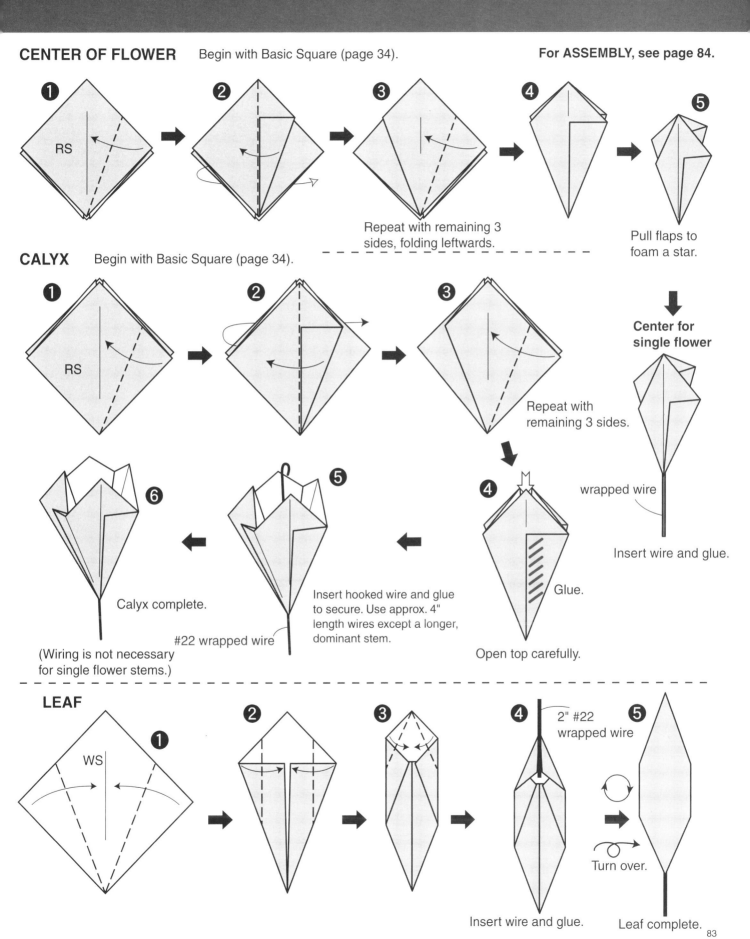

❶ RS

❷

❸ Repeat with remaining 3 sides, folding leftwards.

❹

❺ Pull flaps to foam a star.

CALYX   Begin with Basic Square (page 34).

❶ RS

❷

❸ Repeat with remaining 3 sides.

Center for single flower

wrapped wire

Insert wire and glue.

❹ Glue. Open top carefully.

❺ Insert hooked wire and glue to secure. Use approx. 4" length wires except a longer, dominant stem.

#22 wrapped wire

❻ Calyx complete.

(Wiring is not necessary for single flower stems.)

LEAF

❶ WS

❷

❸

❹ 2" #22 wrapped wire

Insert wire and glue.

❺ Turn over.

Leaf complete.

83

PAPER RATIO

CENTER/
CALYX (¼)

LEAF (⁴⁄₉)

FLORET (1)

FLORET Begin with Basic Pentagon (page 37).

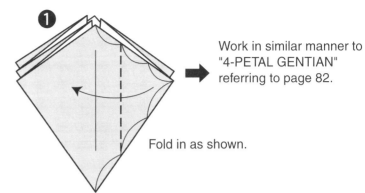

①

Work in similar manner to
"4-PETAL GENTIAN"
referring to page 82.

Fold in as shown.

CENTER OF FLOWER

Begin with Basic Pentagon (page 37).

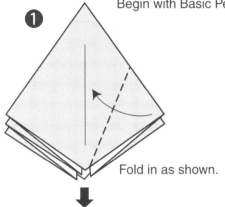

①

Fold in as shown.

CALYX/LEAF: Work in similar manner to
"4-PETAL GENTIAN" referring to page 83.

Work in similar manner to
"4-PETAL GENTIAN"
referring to page 83.

ASSEMBLY

Single flower type

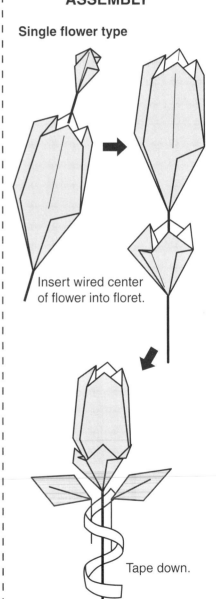

Insert wired center
of flower into floret.

Tape down.

ASSEMBLY

Cluster type

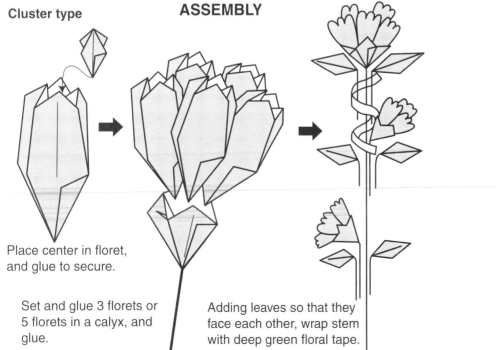

Place center in floret,
and glue to secure.

Set and glue 3 florets or
5 florets in a calyx, and
glue.

Adding leaves so that they
face each other, wrap stem
with deep green floral tape.

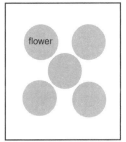

FLOWER

1 RS

petal

Crease.

2

3 Unfold.

4 Using crease, make Inside Reverse Fold.

5

6 A set of 2 petals complete. Make 16 of this.

7 Glue the folds together.

8 Glue 8 pieces together. Make 2 of this, and glue together to form 32 petals in the round.

PAPER RATIO

8 PETALS (1)

LEAF (1/4)

PETAL

SEPAL (1/9 - 1/16)

PETAL

◄ Divide into quarters, then cut each into halves.

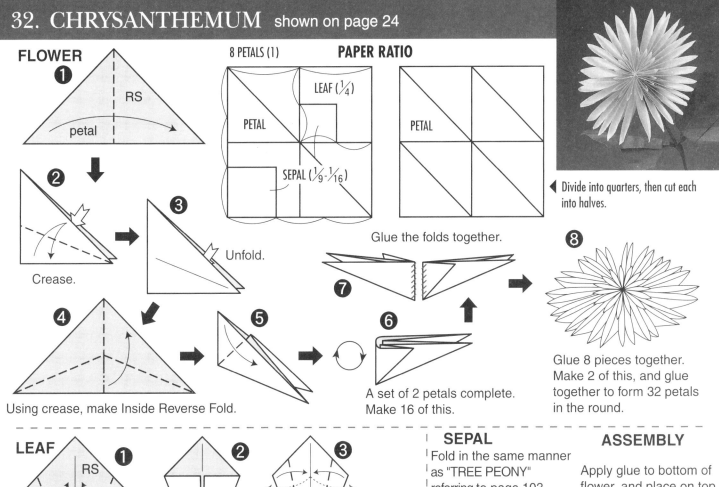

LEAF

1 RS

2

3 Turn over. Pulling out back flap, fold to the middle.

4

5 Form veins by alternating valley and mountain fold.

6

7

8

9

10 approx. 2" #22 wrapped wire
(Omit this if gluing to board.)

11 Leaf complete.

SEPAL

Fold in the same manner as "TREE PEONY" referring to page 103.

Layer 2 sepals.

ASSEMBLY

Apply glue to bottom of flower, and place on top.

Wrap with deep green floral tape. Add leaves facing each other.

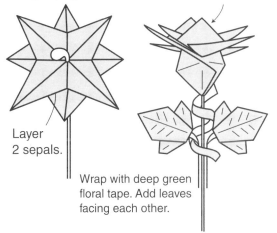
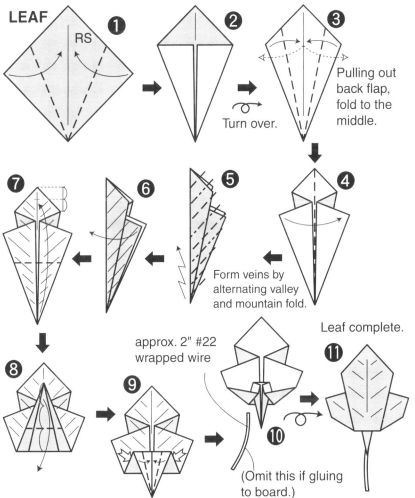

SHIKISHI WALLHANGING

flower

Paper Materials
Flower: 8 or 16 triangles made from 2" squares, cut diagonally in half. Make 5.
Leaf: 3"squares. Make approx. 20.
Sepals: None

Position 5 flowers on *shikishi* card. Fill gaps with leaves.

FLOWER

① Crease crosswise to mark the center point. Fold corners to center.

PAPER RATIO

LEAF (¼)

FLOWER (1)

② Fold in half.

③ Fold in half.

④ Lift and squash-fold leftwards.

⑤

Turn over.

⑥ Lift and squash-fold rightwards.

⑦ Place upside down. Crease as shown.

⑧ Fold corner to the crease just made.

⑨ Fold to the center.

⑩ Repeat behind.

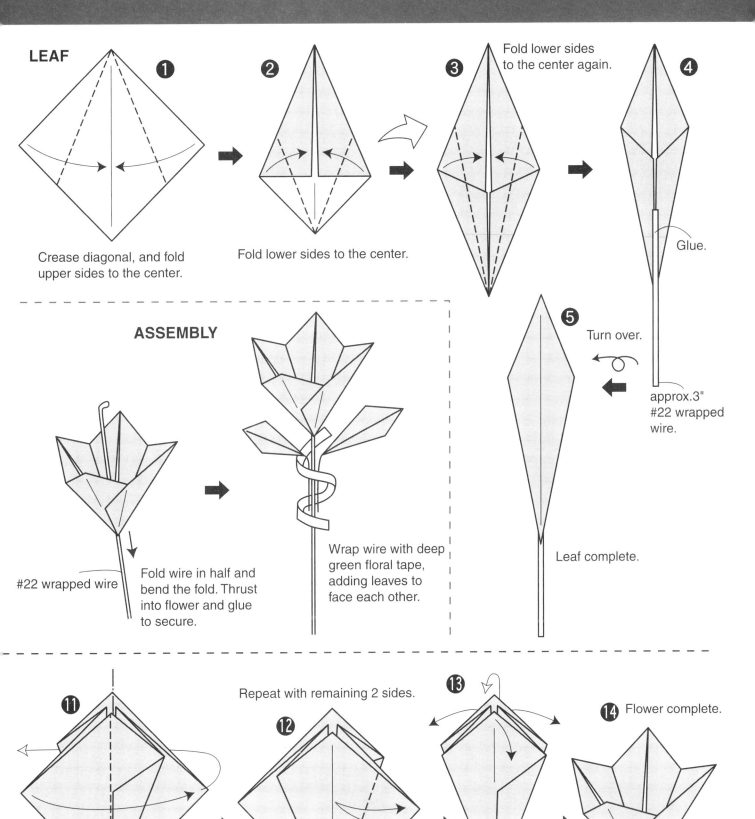

LEAF

① Crease diagonal, and fold upper sides to the center.

② Fold lower sides to the center.

③ Fold lower sides to the center again.

④ Glue.

⑤ Turn over.

approx.3" #22 wrapped wire.

Leaf complete.

ASSEMBLY

#22 wrapped wire

Fold wire in half and bend the fold. Thrust into flower and glue to secure.

Wrap wire with deep green floral tape, adding leaves to face each other.

⑪ Fold over. Repeat behind.

⑫ Repeat with remaining 2 sides.

⑬ Pull the corner outwards.

⑭ Flower complete.

PAPER RATIO

FLOWER (1)

CENTER ($\frac{1}{9}$ X $\frac{1}{2}$)

LEAF ($\frac{1}{4}$)

FLOWER

1 Crease valley fold crosswise, and mountain fold diagonally. Collapse into Basic Square.

RS

Basic Square (page 34)

2

WS

Lift and squash -fold leftwards...

3

...like this. Fold leftwards.

4

Fold to the middle.

5

Turn over.

6

7

8

9

10

11

12

Fold in half.

13

Inside Reverse Fold (page 33)

14

Open out.

15

Flower complete.

LEAF

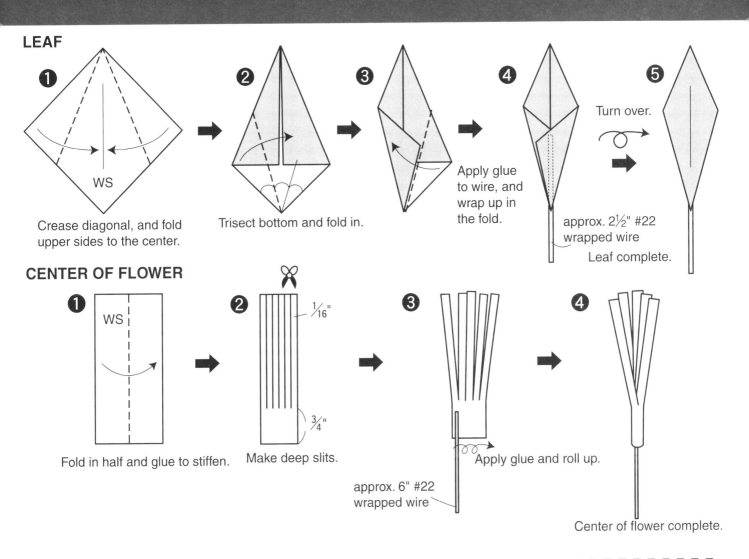

❶ Crease diagonal, and fold upper sides to the center. WS

❷ Trisect bottom and fold in.

❸ Apply glue to wire, and wrap up in the fold.

❹ approx. 2½" #22 wrapped wire

❺ Turn over. Leaf complete.

CENTER OF FLOWER

❶ WS Fold in half and glue to stiffen.

❷ 1/16" 3/4" Make deep slits.

❸ approx. 6" #22 wrapped wire. Apply glue and roll up.

❹ Center of flower complete.

ASSEMBLY

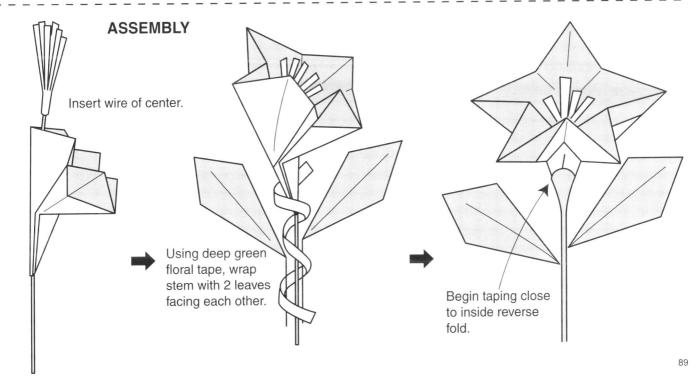

Insert wire of center.

Using deep green floral tape, wrap stem with 2 leaves facing each other.

Begin taping close to inside reverse fold.

FLOWER

Begin with Basic Square (page 34).

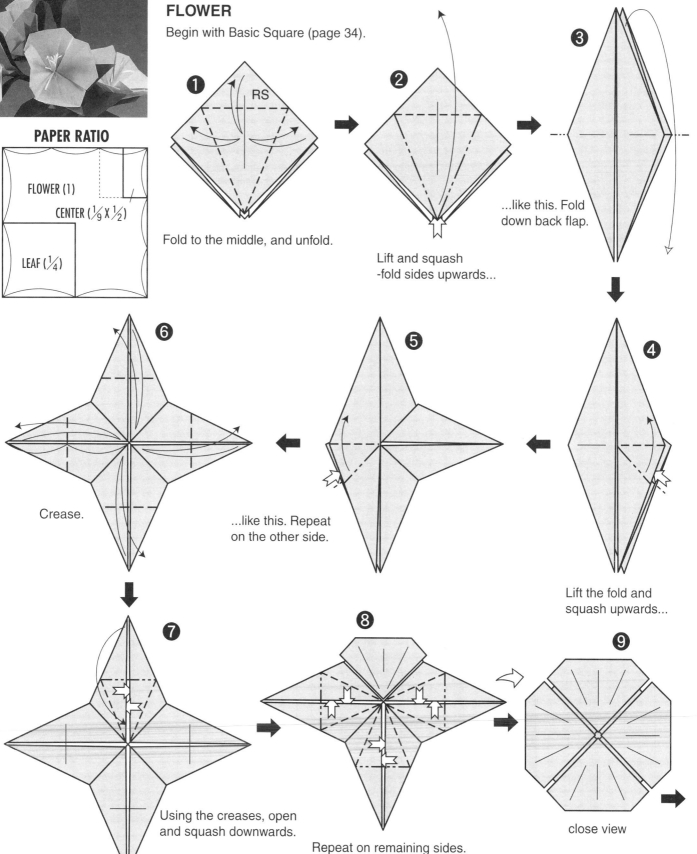

PAPER RATIO

FLOWER (1)

CENTER ($\frac{1}{9}$ X $\frac{1}{2}$)

LEAF ($\frac{1}{4}$)

RS

Fold to the middle, and unfold.

Lift and squash -fold sides upwards...

...like this. Fold down back flap.

Lift the fold and squash upwards...

...like this. Repeat on the other side.

Crease.

Using the creases, open and squash downwards.

Repeat on remaining sides.

close view

LEAF

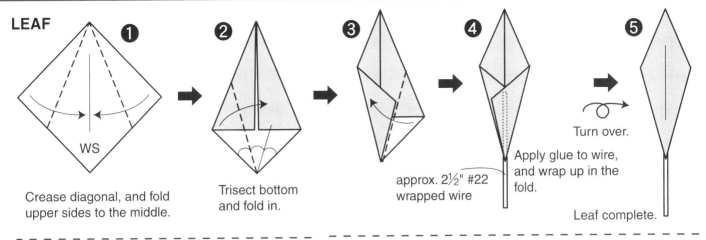

① ② Crease diagonal, and fold upper sides to the middle.

WS

② Trisect bottom and fold in.

③ approx. 2½" #22 wrapped wire

④ Apply glue to wire, and wrap up in the fold.

⑤ Turn over.

Leaf complete.

CENTER OF FLOWER

ASSEMBLY

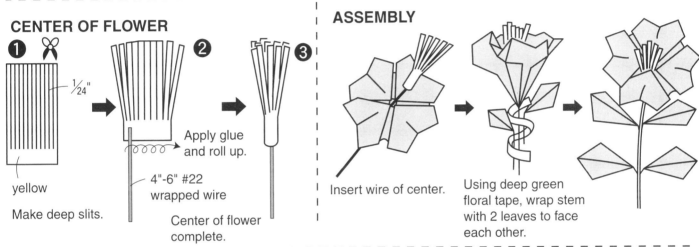

① 1/24"

yellow

Make deep slits.

② Apply glue and roll up.

4"-6" #22 wrapped wire

③ Center of flower complete.

Insert wire of center.

Using deep green floral tape, wrap stem with 2 leaves to face each other.

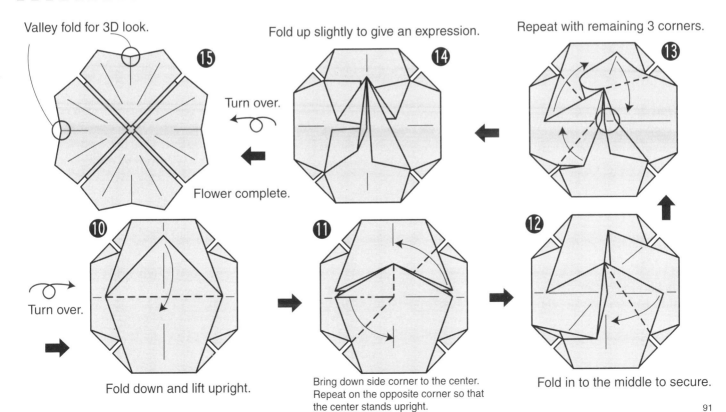

Valley fold for 3D look.

⑮

Turn over.

Flower complete.

Fold up slightly to give an expression.

⑭

Repeat with remaining 3 corners.

⑬

⑫

⑩ Turn over.

Fold down and lift upright.

⑪ Bring down side corner to the center. Repeat on the opposite corner so that the center stands upright.

Fold in to the middle to secure.

34. ADONIS FLOWER shown on page 26

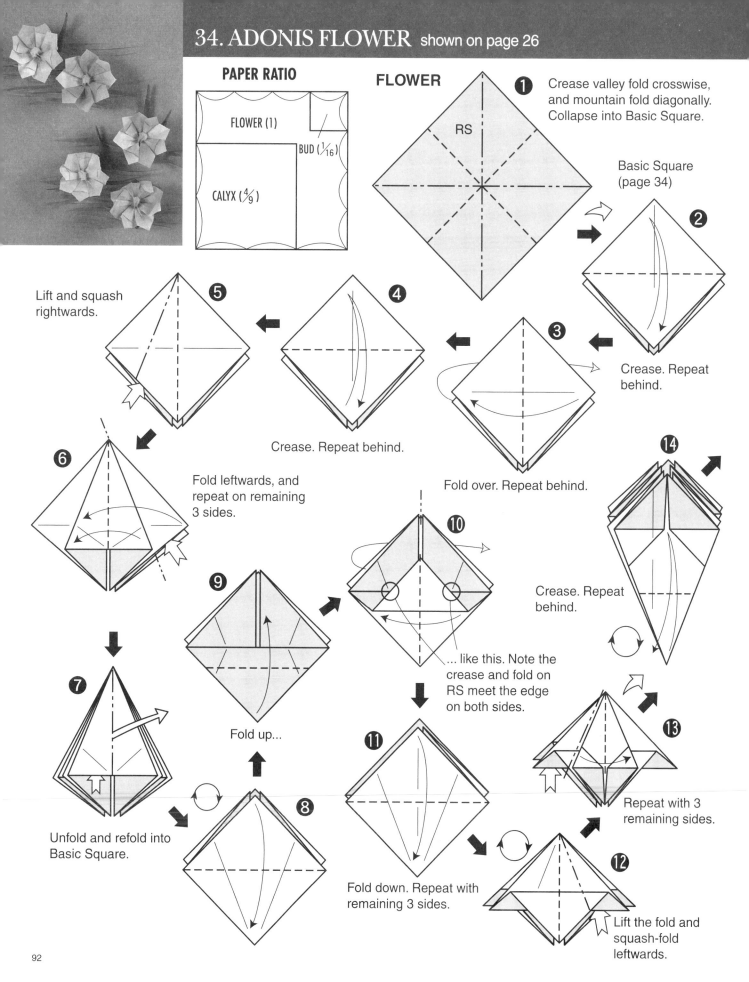

PAPER RATIO

FLOWER (1)

BUD (1/16)

CALYX (4/9)

FLOWER

① Crease valley fold crosswise, and mountain fold diagonally. Collapse into Basic Square.

RS

Basic Square (page 34)

②

③ Crease. Repeat behind.

④ Crease. Repeat behind.

⑤ Lift and squash rightwards.

⑥ Fold leftwards, and repeat on remaining 3 sides.

Fold over. Repeat behind.

⑦ Unfold and refold into Basic Square.

⑧

⑨ Fold up...

⑩ ... like this. Note the crease and fold on RS meet the edge on both sides.

⑪ Fold down. Repeat with remaining 3 sides.

⑫ Lift the fold and squash-fold leftwards.

⑬ Repeat with 3 remaining sides.

⑭ Crease. Repeat behind.

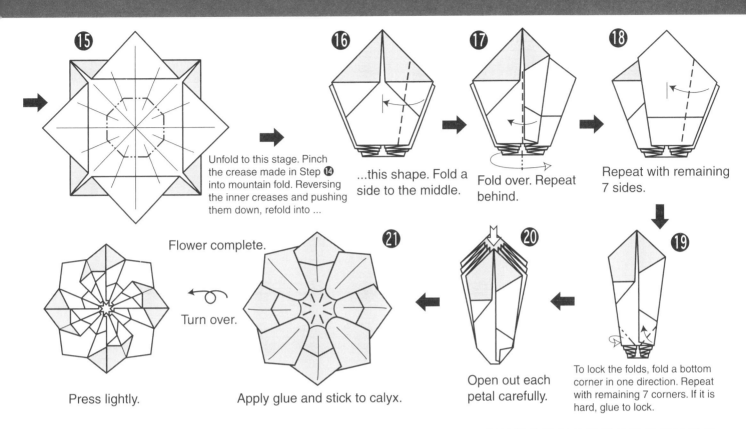

⑮ Unfold to this stage. Pinch the crease made in Step ⑭ into mountain fold. Reversing the inner creases and pushing them down, refold into ...

⑯ ...this shape. Fold a side to the middle.

⑰ Fold over. Repeat behind.

⑱ Repeat with remaining 7 sides.

⑲ To lock the folds, fold a bottom corner in one direction. Repeat with remaining 7 corners. If it is hard, glue to lock.

⑳ Open out each petal carefully.

㉑ Apply glue and stick to calyx.

Flower complete.

Turn over.

Press lightly.

CALYX

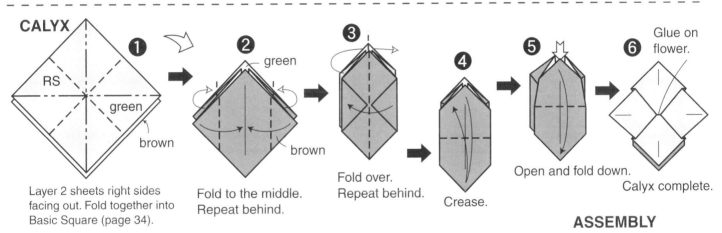

❶ Layer 2 sheets right sides facing out. Fold together into Basic Square (page 34).

RS green brown

❷ green brown
Fold to the middle. Repeat behind.

❸ Fold over. Repeat behind.

❹ Crease.

❺ Open and fold down.

❻ Glue on flower.
Calyx complete.

ASSEMBLY

BUD

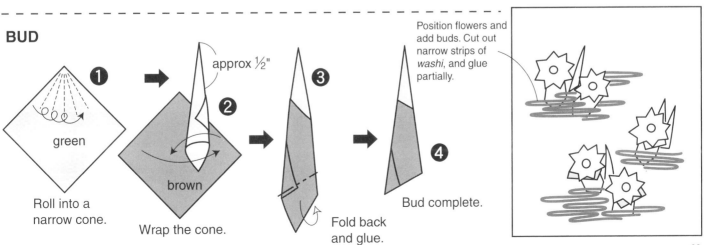

❶ green
Roll into a narrow cone.

❷ approx ½"
brown
Wrap the cone.

❸ Fold back and glue.

❹ Bud complete.

Position flowers and add buds. Cut out narrow strips of *washi*, and glue partially.

93

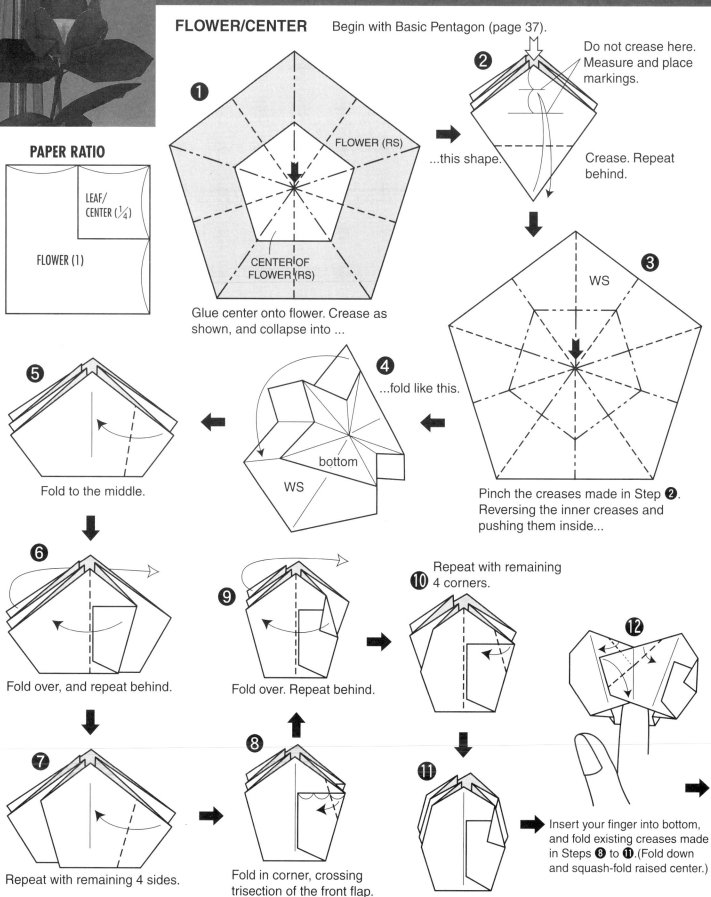

FLOWER/CENTER Begin with Basic Pentagon (page 37).

PAPER RATIO

LEAF/
CENTER (¼)

FLOWER (1)

① FLOWER (RS)

CENTER OF
FLOWER (RS)

Glue center onto flower. Crease as
shown, and collapse into ...

② Do not crease here.
Measure and place
markings.

...this shape.

Crease. Repeat
behind.

③ WS

Pinch the creases made in Step ②.
Reversing the inner creases and
pushing them inside...

④ ...fold like this.

bottom

WS

⑤ Fold to the middle.

⑥ Fold over, and repeat behind.

⑦ Repeat with remaining 4 sides.

⑧ Fold in corner, crossing
trisection of the front flap.

⑨ Fold over. Repeat behind.

⑩ Repeat with remaining
4 corners.

⑪

⑫

Insert your finger into bottom,
and fold existing creases made
in Steps ⑧ to ⑪.(Fold down
and squash-fold raised center.)

LEAF

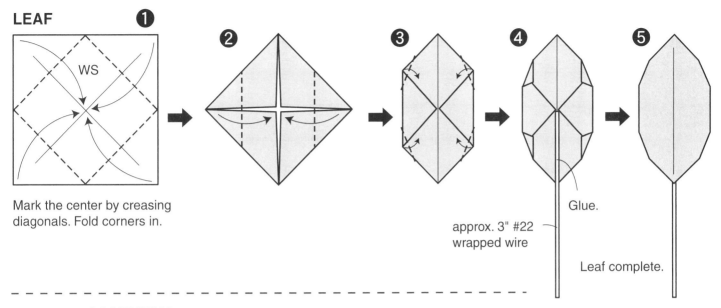

① Mark the center by creasing diagonals. Fold corners in.

②

③

④ approx. 3" #22 wrapped wire — Glue.

⑤ Leaf complete.

ASSEMBLY

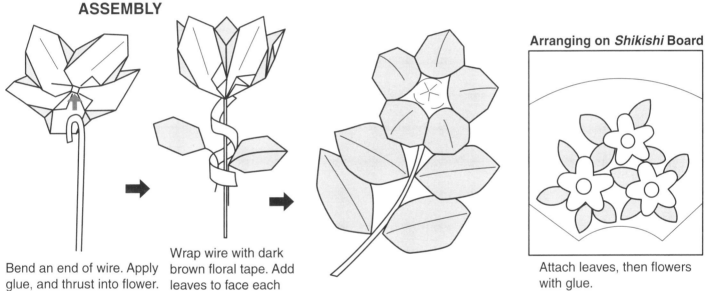

Bend an end of wire. Apply glue, and thrust into flower.

Wrap wire with dark brown floral tape. Add leaves to face each other, and tape down.

Arranging on *Shikishi* Board

Attach leaves, then flowers with glue.

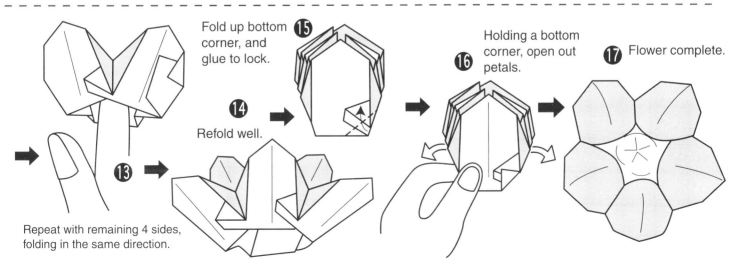

⑬ Repeat with remaining 4 sides, folding in the same direction.

⑭ Refold well.

⑮ Fold up bottom corner, and glue to lock.

⑯ Holding a bottom corner, open out petals.

⑰ Flower complete.

FLOWER

Make Basic Hexagon (page 35), beginning with reverse side of paper. Work until Step ⑰ is done.

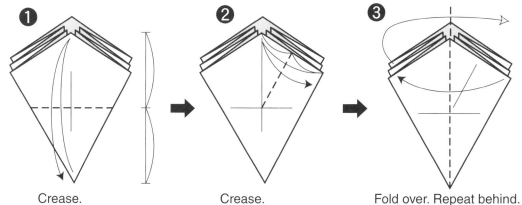

PAPER RATIO

FLOWER (1)
6" square
(example)

7" square (LARGE)
6" square (MEDIUM)
5" square (SMALL)
(example)

LEAF
(Use trisections)

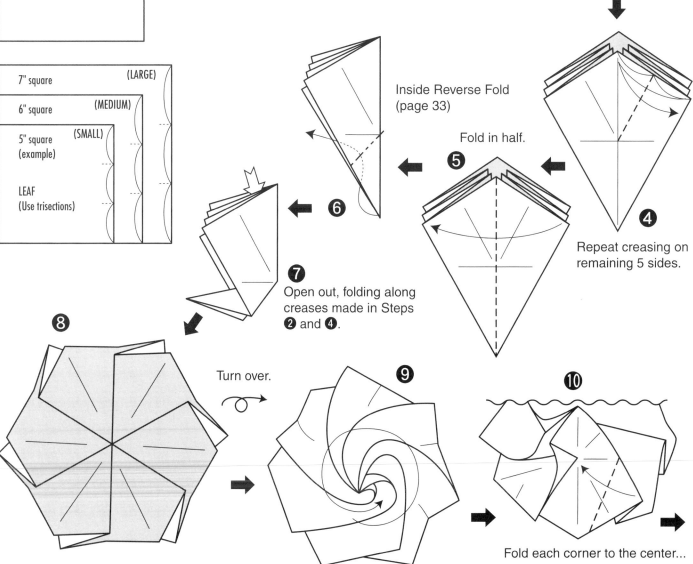

❶ Crease.

❷ Crease.

❸ Fold over. Repeat behind.

Inside Reverse Fold
(page 33)

Fold in half.

❹ Repeat creasing on remaining 5 sides.

❺

❻

❼ Open out, folding along creases made in Steps ❷ and ❹.

❽ Turn over.

❾ Twist the center so that the folds face the same direction.

❿ Fold each corner to the center...

ASSEMBLY

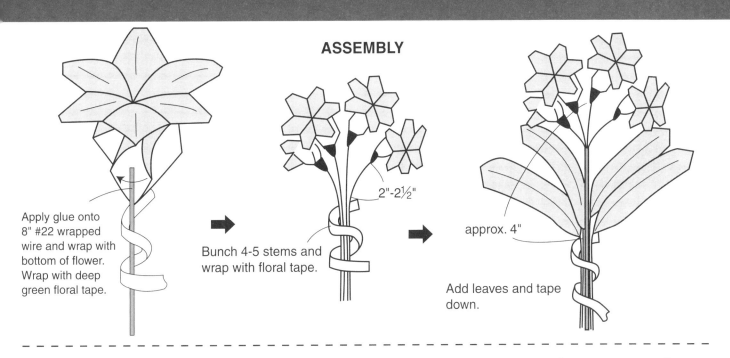

Apply glue onto 8" #22 wrapped wire and wrap with bottom of flower. Wrap with deep green floral tape.

Bunch 4-5 stems and wrap with floral tape.

2"-2½"

approx. 4"

Add leaves and tape down.

LEAF

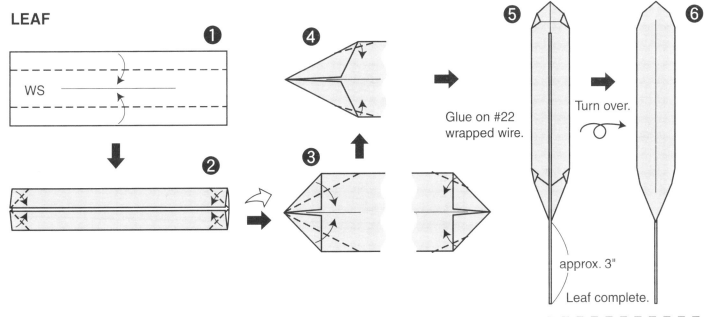

❶

WS

❷

❸

❹

❺ Glue on #22 wrapped wire.

❻ Turn over.

approx. 3"

Leaf complete.

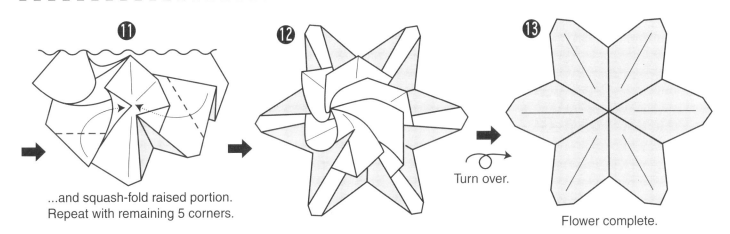

⓫ ...and squash-fold raised portion. Repeat with remaining 5 corners.

⓬

⓭ Turn over.

Flower complete.

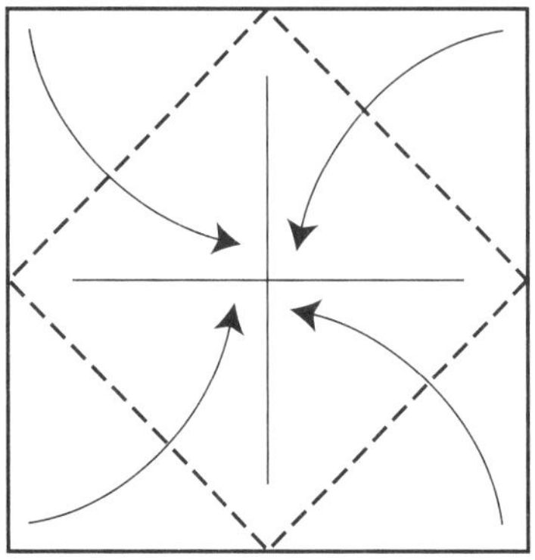

FLOWER

PAPER RATIO

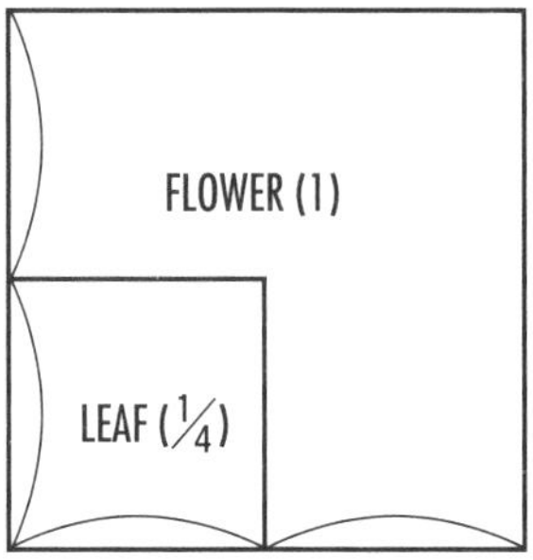

❶

Crease diagonals to mark center. Fold corners to the center.

FLOWER (1)

LEAF ($\frac{1}{4}$)

❷ Fold in half.

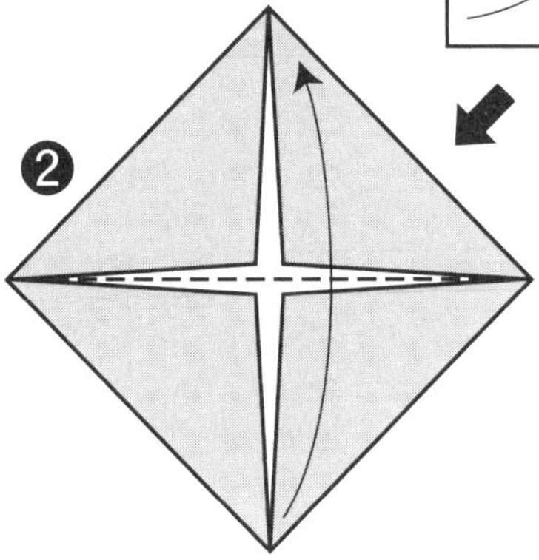

❸ Fold in half.

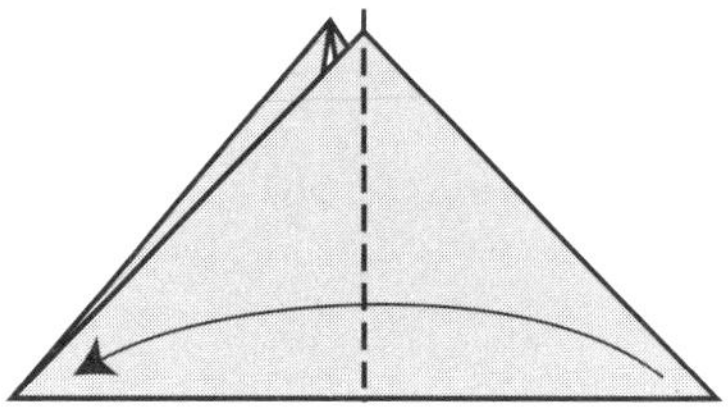

❹ Lift and squash-fold rightwards.

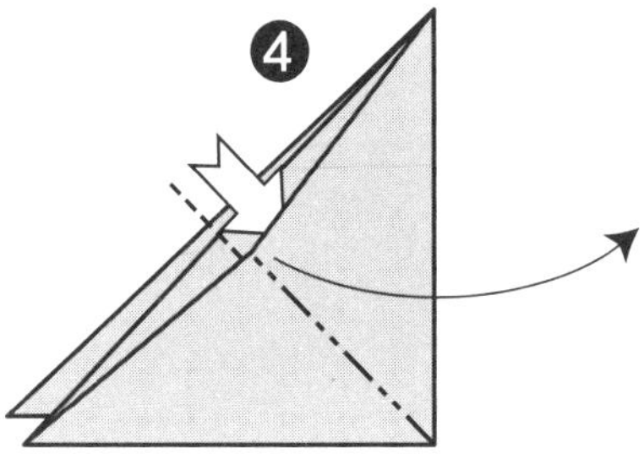

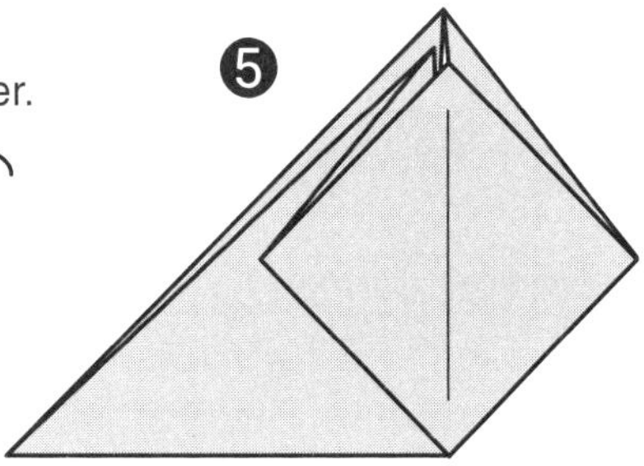

Turn over.

❺

❻

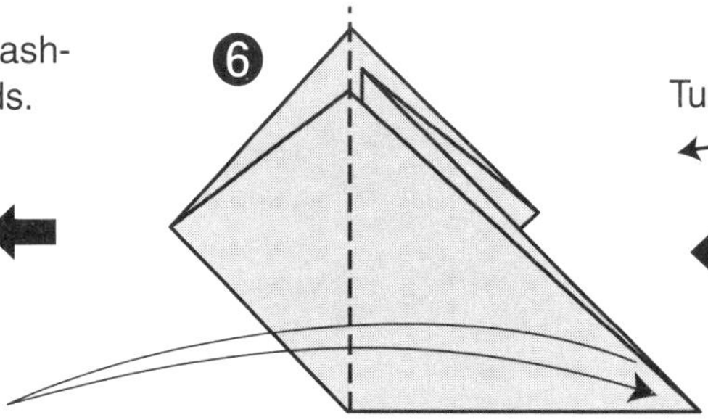

❼ Lift and squash-fold leftwards.

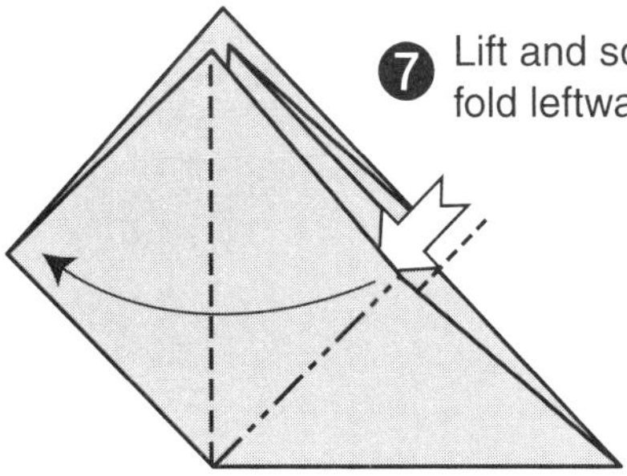

❽ Basic Square (page 34)

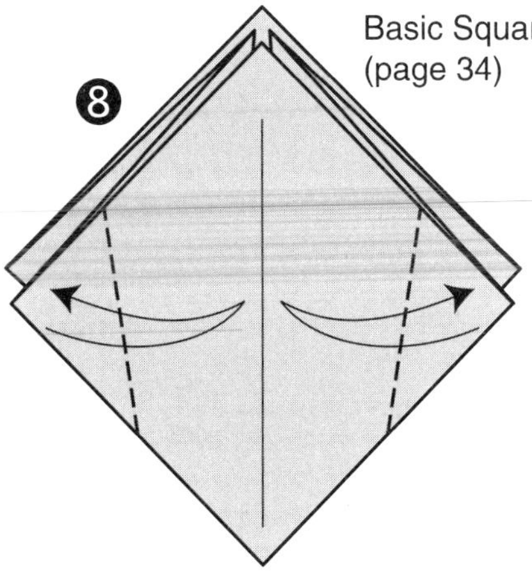

Inside Reverse Fold

❾

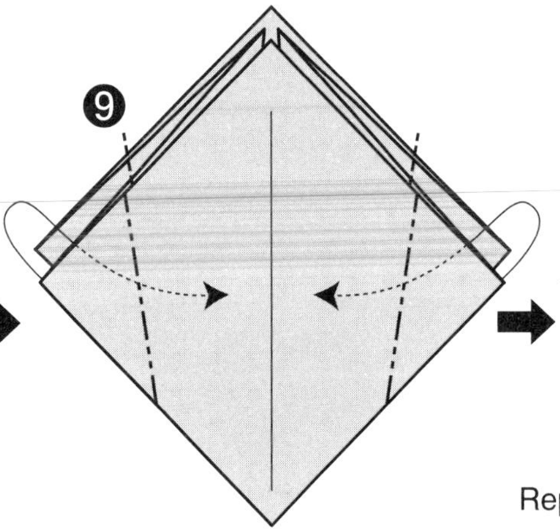

❿ 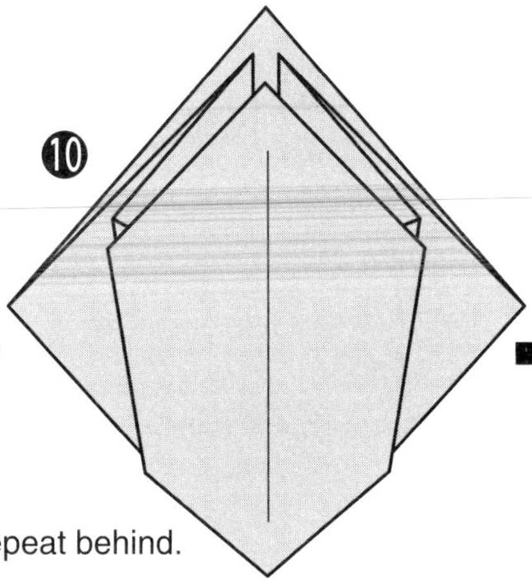 Repeat behind.

LEAF

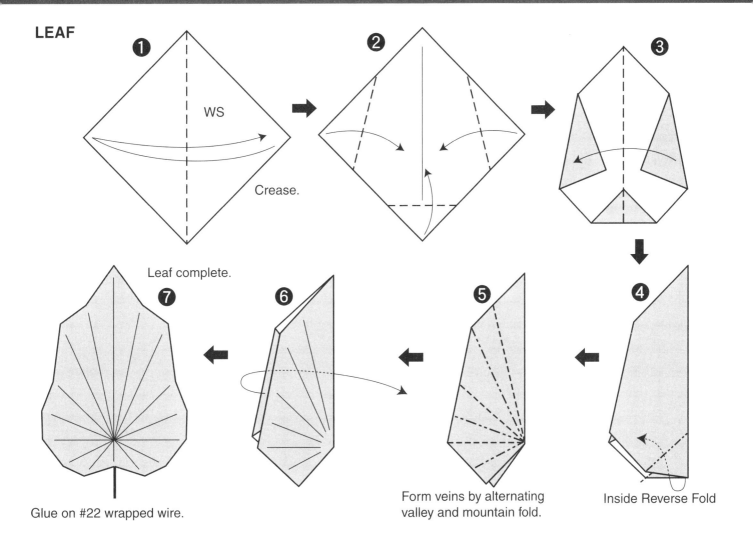

1 WS

Crease.

2

3

4 Inside Reverse Fold

5 Form veins by alternating valley and mountain fold.

6

7 Leaf complete.

Glue on #22 wrapped wire.

ASSEMBLY

11 Fold diagonally...

12 ...like this. Repeat behind.

13 Insert wire with glue. Wrap with dark red floral tape to finish.

Fill a container with florist's foam, and cover with hydroballs. Set leaves so they point outwards. Set flower stems in the middle.

FLOWER

① RS

Crease valley fold crosswise and mountain fold diagonally. Collapse into Basic Square.

②

Basic Square (page 34)

③

PAPER RATIO

FLOWER (1)
6" square
(example)

7" square (LARGE)

6" square (MEDIUM)

5" square (SMALL)
(example)

LEAF

④

⑤

⑥

⑦

⑧

Fold over. Repeat behind.

⑨

Fold to the middle.
Repeat behind.

⑩

Fold over.
Repeat behind.

⑪

⑫

⑬

Match crease with the corner underneath.

Align with the triangle fold.

⑭

Crease.

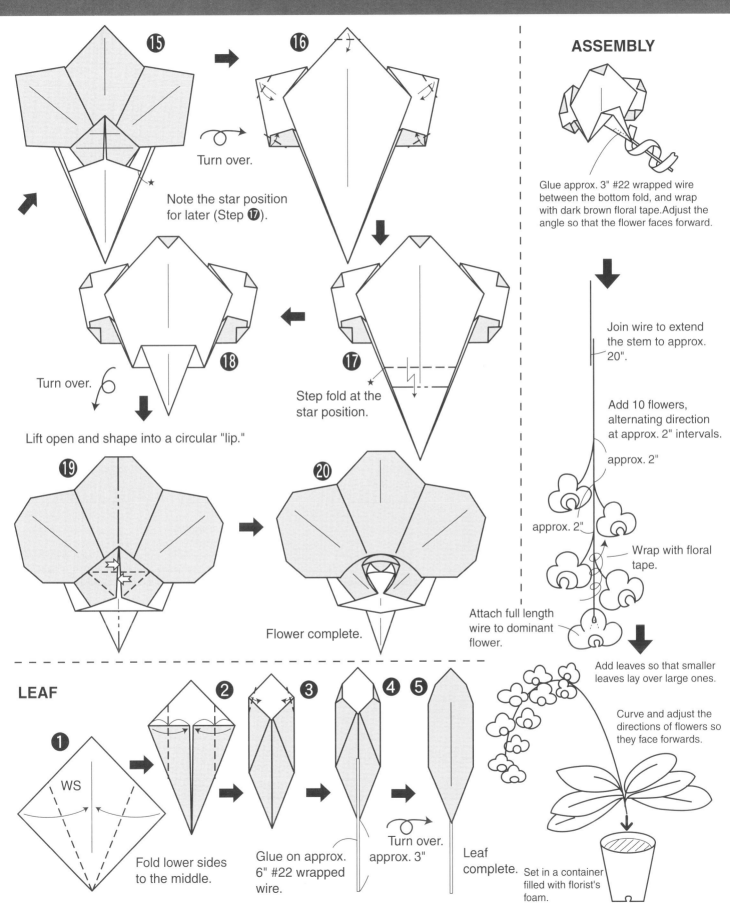

15

Turn over.

Note the star position for later (Step **17**).

16

17

Step fold at the star position.

18

Turn over.

Lift open and shape into a circular "lip."

19

20

Flower complete.

ASSEMBLY

Glue approx. 3" #22 wrapped wire between the bottom fold, and wrap with dark brown floral tape. Adjust the angle so that the flower faces forward.

Join wire to extend the stem to approx. 20".

Add 10 flowers, alternating direction at approx. 2" intervals.

approx. 2"

approx. 2"

Wrap with floral tape.

Attach full length wire to dominant flower.

Add leaves so that smaller leaves lay over large ones.

Curve and adjust the directions of flowers so they face forwards.

Set in a container filled with florist's foam.

LEAF

1

WS

Fold lower sides to the middle.

2

3

Glue on approx. 6" #22 wrapped wire.

4

Turn over. approx. 3"

5

Leaf complete.

37. TREE PEONY shown on page 29

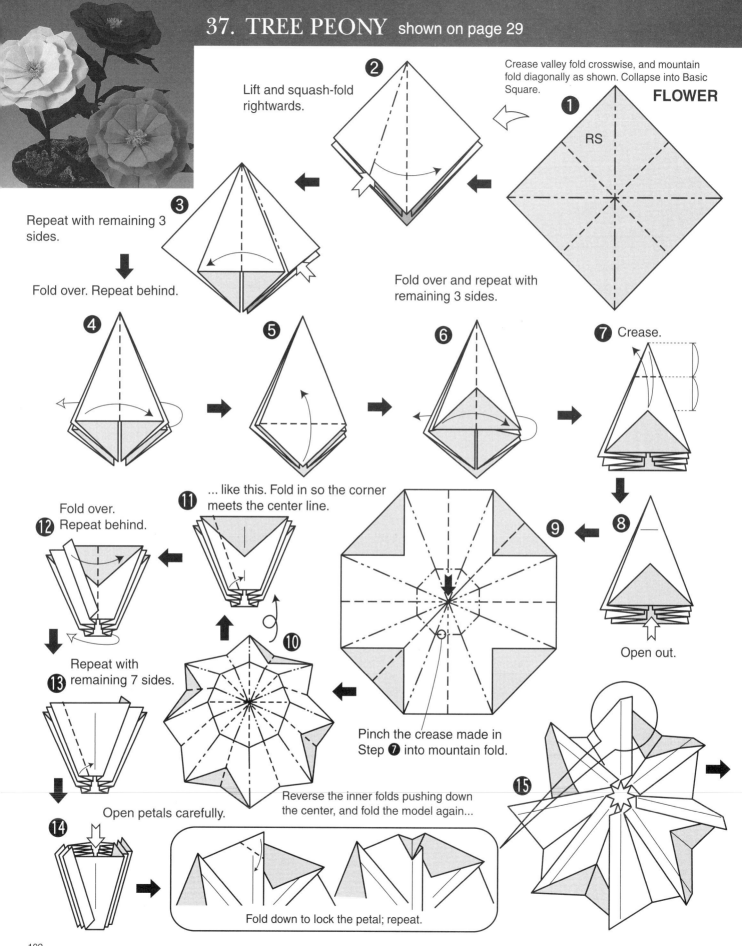

❶ Crease valley fold crosswise, and mountain fold diagonally as shown. Collapse into Basic Square.

FLOWER

RS

❷ Lift and squash-fold rightwards.

❸ Repeat with remaining 3 sides.

Fold over. Repeat behind.

Fold over and repeat with remaining 3 sides.

❹

❺

❻

❼ Crease.

❽ Open out.

❾

❿

Pinch the crease made in Step **❼** into mountain fold.

⓫ ... like this. Fold in so the corner meets the center line.

⓬ Fold over. Repeat behind.

Repeat with remaining 7 sides.

⓭

Reverse the inner folds pushing down the center, and fold the model again...

⓮ Open petals carefully.

Fold down to lock the petal; repeat.

⓯

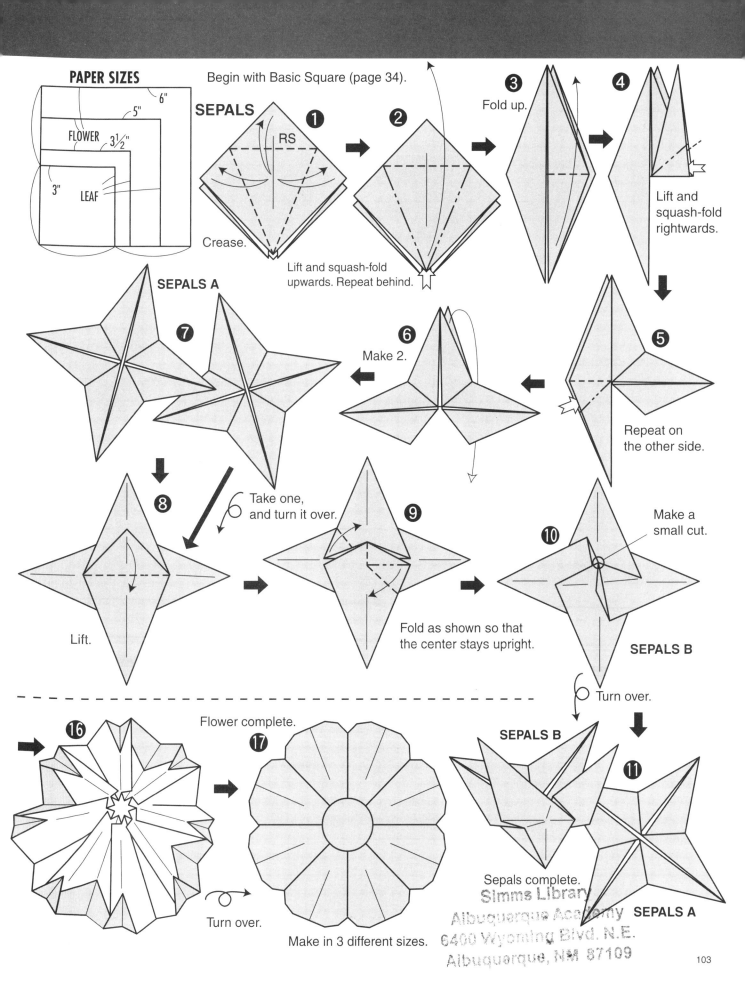

PAPER SIZES

6"
5"
FLOWER 3½"
3"
LEAF

Begin with Basic Square (page 34).

SEPALS

❶ RS

Crease.

❷

Lift and squash-fold upwards. Repeat behind.

❸ Fold up.

❹ Lift and squash-fold rightwards.

❺ Repeat on the other side.

❻ Make 2.

SEPALS A

❼

❽ Lift.

Take one, and turn it over.

❾ Fold as shown so that the center stays upright.

❿ Make a small cut.

SEPALS B

Turn over.

SEPALS B

⓫

Sepals complete.

SEPALS A

⓰

⓱ Flower complete.

Turn over.

Make in 3 different sizes.

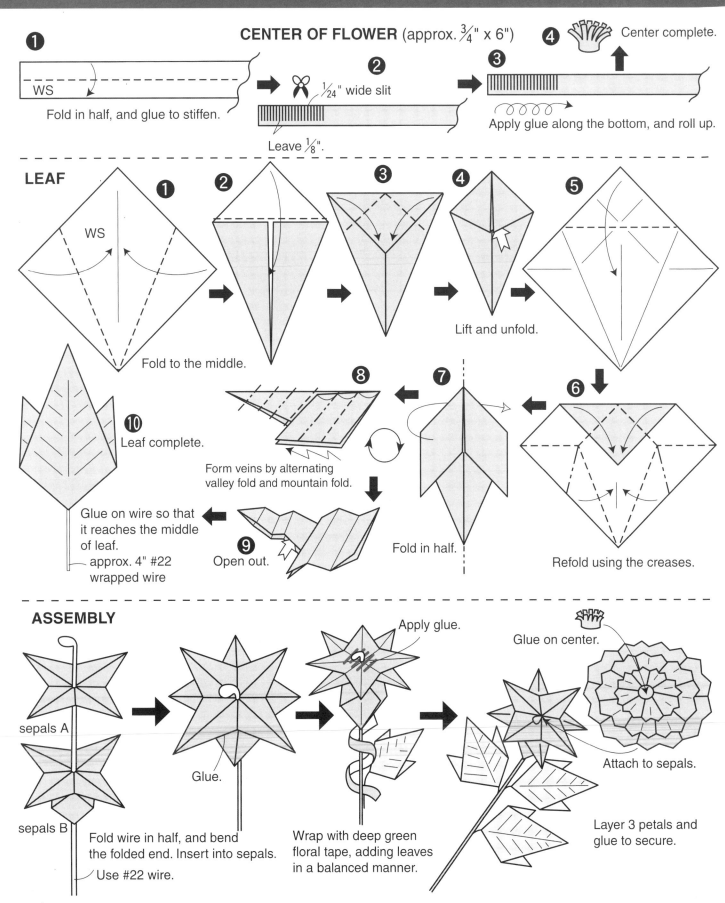

CENTER OF FLOWER (approx. ¾" x 6")

❶ WS
Fold in half, and glue to stiffen.

❷ ½₄" wide slit
Leave ⅛".

❸ Apply glue along the bottom, and roll up.

❹ Center complete.

LEAF

❶ WS
Fold to the middle.

❷

❸

❹ Lift and unfold.

❺

❻ Refold using the creases.

❼ Fold in half.

❽ Form veins by alternating valley fold and mountain fold.

❾ Open out.

❿ Leaf complete.
Glue on wire so that it reaches the middle of leaf.
approx. 4" #22 wrapped wire

ASSEMBLY

sepals A
sepals B
Fold wire in half, and bend the folded end. Insert into sepals.
Use #22 wire.

Glue.

Apply glue.
Wrap with deep green floral tape, adding leaves in a balanced manner.

Glue on center.
Attach to sepals.
Layer 3 petals and glue to secure.

104